Joel, Obadiah, Habakkuk, Zephaniah

Series Editor

Adrian Curtis, University of Manchester, UK

Published in Association with the Society for Old Testament Study

OTHER TITLES IN THE SERIES INCLUDE:

Amos: An Introduction and Study Guide
1 & 2 Kings: An Introduction and Study Guide
1 & 2 Samuel: An Introduction and Study Guide
Ecclesiastes: An Introduction and Study Guide
Exodus: An Introduction and Study Guide
Ezra-Nehemiah: An Introduction and Study Guide
Leviticus: An Introduction and Study Guide
Jeremiah: An Introduction and Study Guide
Job: An Introduction and Study Guide
Joshua: An Introduction and Study Guide
Psalms: An Introduction and Study Guide
Song of Songs: An Introduction and Study Guide
Numbers: An Introduction and Study Guide

T & T CLARK STUDY GUIDES TO THE NEW TESTAMENT:

1 & 2 Thessalonians: An Introduction and Study Guide
1 Peter: An Introduction and Study Guide
2 Corinthians: An Introduction and Study Guide
Colossians: An Introduction and Study Guide
Ephesians: An Introduction and Study Guide
Galatians: An Introduction and Study Guide
Hebrews: An Introduction and Study Guide
James: An Introduction and Study Guide
John: An Introduction and Study Guide
Luke: An Introduction and Study Guide
Mark: An Introduction and Study Guide
Matthew: An Introduction and Study Guide
Philemon: An Introduction and Study Guide
Philippians: An Introduction and Study Guide
Romans: An Introduction and Study Guide
The Acts of the Apostles: An Introduction and Study Guide
The Letters of Jude and Second Peter: An Introduction and Study Guide

Joel, Obadiah, Habakkuk, Zephaniah

An Introduction and

Study Guide

Tchavdar S. Hadjiev

t&tclark

LONDON • NEW YORK • OXFORD • NEW DELHI • SYDNEY

T&T CLARK
Bloomsbury Publishing Plc
50 Bedford Square, London, WC1B 3DP, UK
1385 Broadway, New York, NY 10018, USA

BLOOMSBURY, T&T CLARK and the T&T Clark logo are trademarks of Bloomsbury Publishing Plc

First published in Great Britain 2020

Cover design: Charlotte James

A catalogue record for this book is available from the British Library.

A catalog record for this book is available from the Library of Congress.

ISBN: HB: 978-0-5676-9283-2
PB: 978-0-5676-8046-4
ePDF: 978-0-5676-8048-8
eBook: 978-0-5676-8047-1

Typeset by Deanta Global Publishing Services, Chennai, India

To find out more about our authors and books visit www.bloomsbury.com and sign up for our newsletters.

Contents

Series preface vii
Abbreviations ix

Introduction 1

1 **Joel, Obadiah, Habakkuk, Zephaniah and the book of the Twelve** 6

Part One Joel

2 **Reading Joel as a composite literary work: The structure and unity of the book** 13

3 **The contexts of Joel: Historical, literary and canonical** 19

4 **The setting and genre of Joel** 24

5 **Locusts, armies and the Day of the Lord in the book of Joel** 31

Part Two Obadiah

6 **The composition and unity of the book of Obadiah** 41

7 **The historical background of Obadiah** 45

8 **The genre, setting and purpose of Obadiah** 49

9 **Edom and the image of the other** 52

Part Three Habakkuk

10 **Interpretation problems in the book of Habakkuk** 59

11 **The righteous and the wicked: The contexts and meaning of Habakkuk 1–2** 65

12 **The prayer of Habakkuk (chapter 3)** 73

13 **Theodicy, empire and violence: Reflections on the theology of Habakkuk** 79

Part Four Zephaniah

14 **The genre and structures of the book of Zephaniah** 89

15 **Zephaniah the prophet** 97

16 **Zephaniah's oracles against the nations and the composition of 1.1–3.8** 107

17 **Zephaniah's message of hope (3.9-20) and the canonical shape of the book** 115

Bibliography 123
General subject index 140
Index of scripture references 142

Series preface

How can a potential reader be sure that a Guide to a biblical book is balanced and reliable? One answer is 'If the Guide has been produced under the auspices of an organisation such as the Society for Old Testament Study.'

Founded in 1917, the Society for Old Testament Study (or SOTS as it is commonly known) is a British and Irish society for Old Testament scholars, but with a world-wide membership. It seeks to foster the academic study of the Old Testament/Hebrew Bible in various ways, for example by arranging Conferences (usually twice per year) for its members, maintaining links with other learned societies with similar interests in the British Isles and abroad, and producing a range of publications, including scholarly monographs, and collections of essays by individual authors or on specific topics. Periodically it has published volumes seeking to provide an overview of recent developments and emphases in the discipline at the time of publication. The annual *Society for Old Testament Study Book List*, containing succinct reviews by members of the Society of works on the Old Testament and related areas which have been published in the previous year or so, has proved an invaluable bibliographical resource.

With the needs of students in particular in mind, the Society also produced a series of Study Guides to the books of the Old Testament. This first series of Old Testament Guides, published for the Society by Sheffield Academic Press in the 1980s and 1990s, under the general editorship of the late Professor Norman Whybray, was well received as a very useful resource which teachers could recommend to their students with confidence. But it has inevitably become dated with the passage of time, hence the decision that a new series should be commissioned.

The aim of the new series is to continue the tradition established by the first Series, namely to provide a concise, comprehensive, manageable and affordable guide to each biblical book. The intention is that each volume will contain an authoritative overview of the current thinking on the traditional matters of Old Testament/Hebrew Bible introduction, addressing matters of content, major critical issues, and theological perspectives, in the light of recent scholarship, and suggesting suitable further reading. Where appropriate to the particular biblical book or books, attention may also be given to less traditional approaches or particular theoretical perspectives.

All the authors are members of the Society, known for their scholarship and with wide experience of teaching in Universities and Colleges. The series general editor, Adrian Curtis, taught Old Testament/Hebrew Bible at the University of Manchester for many years, is a former Secretary of the Society, and was President of the Society for 2016.

It is the hope of the Society that these Guides will stimulate in their readers an appreciation of the body of literature whose study is at the heart of all its activities.

Abbreviations

AB	Anchor Bible
ANE	Ancient Near East
ANET	*Ancient Near Eastern Texts Relating to the Old Testament*. J.B. Pritchard (ed.), Princeton: Princeton University Press, 1969
ATD	Das Alte Testament Deutsch
ANEM	Ancient Near Eastern Monographs
BDB	F. Brown, S.R. Driver, C.A. Briggs, *Hebrew and English Lexicon*. Oxford: Oxford University Press, 1907
BZ	*Biblische Zeitschrift*
BZAW	Beihefte zur Zeitschrift für die alttestamentliche Wissenschaft
BIS	Biblical Interpretation Series
COS	*The Context of Scripture: Canonical Compositions, Monumental Inscriptions, and Archival Documents from the Biblical World*. W.W. Hallo and K.L. Younger, Jr. (eds), Leiden and Boston: Brill, 2003
CSHB	Critical Studies in the Hebrew Bible
CBQ	*Catholic Biblical Quarterly*
CBR	*Currents in Biblical Research*
CR: BS	*Currents in Research: Biblical Studies*
ESV	English Standard Version
HALOT	*The Hebrew and Aramaic Lexicon of the Old Testament: The new Koehler-Baumgartner in English*, 5 vols. L. Koehler and W. Baumgartner. Leiden, New York and Köln: Brill, 1994.
HCOT	Historical Commentary of the Old Testament
FRLANT	Forschungen zur Religion und Literatur des Alten und Neuen Testaments
ICC	International Critical Commentary
ITC	International Theological Commentary

JBL	*Journal of Biblical Literature*
JHS	*Journal of Hebrew Scriptures*
JSOT	*Journal for the Study of the Old Testament*
JSOTSUP	Journal for the Study of the Old Testament Supplementary Series
JTS	*Journal of Theological Studies*
KAT	Kommentar zum Alten Testament
LHBOTS	Library of Hebrew Bible/Old Testament Study
NICOT	New International Commentary on the Old Testament
NRSV	New Revised Standard Version
NSKAT	Neuer Stuttgarter Kommentar Altes Testament
NT	New Testament
OAN	Oracles against the nations
OT	Old Testament
OTL	Old Testament Library
OTE	*Old Testament Essays*
SBLDS	Society of Biblical Literature Dissertation Series
SBLMS	Society of Biblical Literature Monograph Series
SBLSS	Society of Biblical Literature Symposium Series
SAA	State Archives of Assyria (see Parpola 1997)
VTSUP	Supplements to Vetus Testamentum
VT	*Vetus Testamentum*
WMANT	Wissenschaftliche Monographien zum Alten und Neuen Testament
WBC	Word Biblical Commentary
ZAW	*Zeitschrift für die alttestamentliche Wissenschaft*
*	Against a biblical reference, this indicates that only parts of the passage are referred to.

Introduction

Chapter Outline

Commentaries on Joel, Obadiah, Habakkuk, Zephaniah   2

The books of Joel, Obadiah, Habakkuk, and Zephaniah belong to what are often thought to be the more obscure parts of the Hebrew Bible. Yet, they introduce us to many of the central issues related to the study of OT prophecy and its central themes. In terms of contents these books deal with topics that stand at the core of biblical prophecy: idolatry and injustice, judgement in the form of military and natural disasters, repentance, relationships with foreign nations, theodicy and faith, divine intervention, salvation and renewal of the world. They are also some of the principal texts where the concept of the Day of the Lord is developed at length. Their theology raises important ethical and existential questions like how to deal with the 'other', how to think about human and divine violence and how to cope with the inexplicable mystery of the world. Considered from a historical point of view, Joel, Obadiah, Habakkuk, and Zephaniah afford insights into the relationship between prophecy, cult and politics, the role of scribes in the production of prophetic literature, the oral and written means of proclamation of the prophetic message, intertextuality and the reuse of earlier traditions.

This study deals with the four Minor Prophets in turn. It does not follow the exact same pattern for each one of them because the books present different sets of issues, but it discusses the key literary, historical and hermeneutical questions every reader needs to address. First is the question of genre and literary shape. What are these prophetic books and what should we expect from reading them? Are they unified or composite literary works and does this make a difference to the way we read? How do their structures and literary characteristics shape our understanding? Second is the question of context. Should we look to the historical or the canonical context as the appropriate guide of our interpretation? If the former, what exactly is this context and can we identify it with any measure of certainty? Finally, the Minor Prophets present the modern reader with various hermeneutical challenges. On the basis of decisions about genre and context, how do we construe their theology and major themes? How do we relate those themes to contemporary debates and concerns?

Commentaries on Joel, Obadiah, Habakkuk, Zephaniah

(for full details see the bibliography, pp. 123–139)

Allen 1976 (Joel, Obadiah): useful exegetical discussion and summary of previous scholarship.

Andersen 2001 (Habakkuk): a major commentary primarily interested in the literary and poetic aspects of the text; relates the whole book to the historical prophet.

Assis 2013 (Joel): argues that Joel was composed during the exilic period and reading it against this historical background is crucial for its correct interpretation.

Barker/Bailey 1998 (Habakkuk, Zephaniah): takes a conservative approach, contains a fair amount of exegetical detail and some engagement with the Hebrew, but accessible to the non-specialist.

Berlin 1994 (Zephaniah): a literary, final-form approach with detailed textual notes.

Barton 2001 (Joel and Obadiah): one of the best modern commentaries written from a historical-critical perspective.

Ben Zvi 1991, 1996a (Zephaniah, Obadiah): detailed notes focused on linguistic and literary issues and a commentary informed by the view that the books are scribal compositions from the post-monarchic period.

Block 2017 (Obadiah): a clearly written commentary from a conservative perspective; offers a rhetorical analysis of the book.

Boadt 1982 (Habakkuk, Zephaniah): an exegetical commentary with an interest in historical issues.

Bruckner 2004 (Habakkuk, Zephaniah): a non-technical commentary that seeks to bridge the historical and contemporary contexts.

Coggins 1985 (Obadiah) 2000 (Joel): shorter commentaries that pay attention to the poetic qualities, intertextual allusions and the difficulties of the Hebrew text.

Crenshaw 1995 (Joel): A major commentary with a useful introduction and a wealth of exegetical detail.

Dahmen 2001 (Joel): an informative exegetical commentary with an interest in intertextual connections that avoids technical issues and has a concluding chapter on reception history (in German).

Dangl 2014 (Habakkuk): accessible and non-technical commentary with an eye of the theology and reception of the text (in German).

Dietrich 2016 (Habakkuk, Zephaniah): combines synchronic and diachronic approaches to the prophetic text, plus some brief textual comments.

Ferreiro 2003 (Joel, Obadiah, Habakkuk, Zephaniah): not a traditional commentary but a compendium of comments from early Christian writers designed to give readers a glimpse into aspects of the reception history of the prophetic books.

Floyd 2000 (Habakkuk, Zephaniah): provides illuminating discussions of structure and genre, and how those relate to the meaning of the text.

Gafney 2017 (Habakkuk, Zephaniah): good exegetical discussion accessible to the non-specialist, with some interesting contextual reflections.

Garrett 1997 (Joel): a well-informed exegetical commentary with several excursuses that seek to relate the text more overtly to the concerns of a Christian readership.

Hubbard 1989 (Joel): brief, accessible, very useful for the non-specialist.

Irsigler 2002 (Zephaniah): a major historical-critical commentary, a must for any serious student of the book (in German).

Jenson 2008 (Obadiah): a brief final-form commentary with an eye to the theological dimensions of the text.

Jeremias 2007 (Joel, Obadiah): a short and useful exegetical commentary from one of the leading scholars on the Minor Prophets (in German).

Niehaus 1993 (Obadiah): contains an exegetical section dealing with the Hebrew text, followed by an exposition.

Nogalski 2011 (Joel, Obadiah, Habakkuk, Zephaniah): a well-written and well laid-out commentary with some insightful reflections on the contemporary relevance of the text; based on the author's conviction that the individual prophecies are part of the larger book of the Twelve.

O'Brien 2004 (Habakkuk, Zephaniah): a final-form approach, focusing on literary and exegetical issues with an eye to the theological dimensions of the text.

Ogden 1987 (Joel): a brief commentary interpreting the book against the background of a lament liturgy.

Perlitt 2004 (Habakkuk, Zephaniah): useful exegetical discussion which sees the books as collections of heterogeneous materials (in German).

Raabe 1996 (Obadiah): a very detailed commentary with lengthy introduction and discussions of individual words and phrases.

Renkema 2003 (Obadiah): detailed and useful exegetical commentary.

Roberts 1991 (Habakkuk, Zephaniah): brief but informative exegetical discussion and textual notes.

Robertson 1990 (Habakkuk, Zephaniah): a detailed exegetical commentary from a conservative perspective.

Rudolph 1971 (Joel, Obadiah), 1975 (Habakkuk, Zephaniah): detailed exegesis and textual notes, still well worth consulting (in German).

Seybold 1991 (Habakkuk, Zephaniah): a relatively brief redaction-critical commentary (in German).

Seitz 2016 (Joel): adopts a canonical approach and is especially interested in the theological contribution of Joel.

Smith 1984 (Habakkuk, Zephaniah): a brief commentary which introduces some of the exegetical issues.

Stuart 1987 (Joel, Obadiah): written from a conservative perspective, contains some useful information.

Sweeney 2000a (Joel, Obadiah, Habakkuk, Zephaniah): treats the final-form of the text on the assumption that it reflects the ministry of the historical prophets, many of whom come from the pre-exilic period.

Sweeney 2003a (Zephaniah): an important commentary which interprets the whole book against the historical background of Josiah's reign.

Szeles 1987 (Habakkuk, Zephaniah): a standard exegetical commentary which touches upon the difficulties of the Hebrew text in a way that is accessible to the non-specialist.

Thomas 2018 (Habakkuk): a final-form commentary interested in the interrelationship between biblical studies and systematic theology.

Vlaardingerbroek 1999 (Zephaniah): a detailed, informative and balanced treatment of the text.

Wolff 1977 (Joel) 1986 (Obadiah): careful exegetical work from one of the leading form and redaction-critical scholars on the Minor Prophets; a good starting place for an in-depth study.

1

Joel, Obadiah, Habakkuk, Zephaniah and the book of the Twelve

Chapter Outline

The book of the Twelve hypothesis   6
Evaluating the hypothesis   8
Conclusion   9
Further study   10

The book of the Twelve hypothesis

During most of the twentieth century scholars aimed to read the books of the Minor Prophets primarily against the background of their presumed original historical context. Zephaniah and Habakkuk were usually interpreted against the background of Judah in the late monarchic period (seventh century BCE), during the reigns of Josiah and Jehoiakim. Obadiah was usually placed in the exilic period (sixth century BCE) and Joel in post-exilic times (fifth or fourth century BCE). A good example of this approach can be found in the classic *History of Prophecy in Israel* by Blenkinsopp (1996).

Over the last three decades a major shift has occurred in this respect. The idea of the 'book of the Twelve' arrived in full force on the academic scene. According to this hypothesis the scrolls of the Minor Prophets right from the start were incorporated into a single literary work and were read and redacted with the other prophetic texts in mind. This way of understanding the compositional history of the Twelve has implications for the way in which the individual 'books' are to be read. Instead of the putative *historical* contexts of the prophets' proclamation, or of the first writing and subsequent redaction of their oracles, scholars now tend to look primarily to the *literary* context of the Twelve as providing us with the appropriate reference point for understanding the prophetic word.

The particulars of this compositional history are reconstructed in different ways. Nogalski (1993a,b) suggests that there were some 'literary precursors' to the book of the Twelve: a book of the Four prophets (Hosea, Amos, Micah and Zephaniah) and a Haggai-Zechariah corpus. The decisive step in the formation of the Twelve was a 'Joel-related layer' in which a redactor incorporated these precursors with Joel, Obadiah, Nahum, Habakkuk and Malachi and heavily edited the newly created work to form a single composition. In German scholarship this process is seen as a much more complicated affair. Both Schart (1998) and Wöhrle (2006, 2008a) accept the existence of a book of the Four, but postulate a number of editions between it and the final form of the Twelve. In Schart's opinion first Nahum and Habakkuk were added, then Haggai and Zechariah, then Joel and Obadiah, each of those resulting in redactional insertions in the already existing corpus. Wöhrle argues that at an early stage Hosea was removed from the beginning of the book of the Four and was replaced by Joel. This reshaped book of the Four was joined to Haggai-Zechariah (and Nahum) and the newly created composition underwent several redactions before Hosea was reintroduced as the opening section of the book of the Twelve. Bosshard-Nepustil (1997) proposes an entirely different model. During the exilic period early versions of Joel, Habakkuk and Zephaniah were added to Hosea, Amos, Micah and Nahum and subsequently edited to parallel the redactional developments of the book of Isaiah.

Whatever the precise details of the reconstructed compositional history, the adoption of such an approach impacts the way these prophetic books are interpreted. For example, Nogalski (2000) terms Joel the 'literary anchor' of the Twelve and argues that it is meant to be read not independently but with the rest of the Minor Prophets in mind. It introduces key motifs like fertility, Judah and Jerusalem and the Day of the Lord that resurface later and unify the collection. The book offers a 'historical paradigm' centred around the themes of disaster, repentance, restoration and judgement of enemy nations that is meant to serve as an interpretative prism through which the rest of the Minor Prophets are to be read. This paradigm provides an explanation for the shape of the history that is to unfold in the Twelve and a hope for its final outcome.

According to Everson (2003) the book of the Twelve in its totality presents the reader with a 'theology of history' which understands the Assyrian, Babylonian and Persian periods as a series of 'days of Yahweh': historical crises in which Yahweh's kingship and presence were manifested in particular ways. Within that scheme Habakkuk is a reflection on the tragic death of Josiah in 609 BCE coming straight after the 'day of Yahweh' manifested in the demise of Assyria, depicted in Nahum. Habakkuk contributes to the Twelve's theology of history by focusing on a period of disillusionment when, in contrast to the 'days of Yahweh', God's intervention and blessing were not immediately apparent. Its contribution consists of the call to remain faithful through the difficult times of uncertainty and suffering.

Evaluating the hypothesis

Two types of evidence, external and internal, support the existence of a 'book of the Twelve', according to the proponents of this theory: First, manuscript evidence and references in ancient sources suggest that the first recipients of the books of the Minor Prophets regarded them as integral parts of a single whole (Nogalski 1993a: 2–3; Jones 1995: 8; Fuller 1996; Schart 1998: 4). Second, careful analysis of the text demonstrates that the Twelve exhibit a number of literary interconnections. Exploration of these connections forms an important part of the work of Nogalski, Schart, Bosshard-Nepustil and Wöhrle, reviewed above. The existence of such links, in their view, suggests a deliberate effort to bind the prophetic scripts together. The careful reader will pick up the numerous allusions and interpret the various parts of the collection in light of each other.

Not everyone, however, has been convinced by this approach (Ben Zvi 1996c, 2009b; Beck 2005; Hadjiev 2009: 7–40; Renz 2018). The fact that towards the end of the first millennium BCE the Twelve were copied onto a single scroll and sometimes referred to as a single entity does not tell us very much. It shows that eventually the twelve independent scripts of the Minor Prophets were brought together in an anthology type collection (Beck 2006), but does not necessarily throw any light on the process of their composition or the intentions of the editors responsible for the final form of their books (Hadjiev 2020). The alleged interconnections between the books of the

Minor Prophets are an even less secure basis on which to build such a theory. Sometimes the appearance of shared vocabulary is simply a coincidence. On other occasions there are unmistakable literary allusions, but their role is not to suggest to the reader that the different books of the Minor Prophets form a single composition (Ben Zvi 1996c: 135–42; Hadjiev 2010, 2020; Renz 2018).

Moreover, some textual features point in the exact opposite direction, that the Minor Prophets are to be read separately, not together. Unlike the books of Isaiah, Jeremiah and Ezekiel, the putative 'book of the Twelve' is not unified by means of a single prophetic figure, or a common title. If anything, by attributing the prophetic material to different individuals from different historical periods, the superscriptions of the various Minor Prophets create the impression that these are independent works (Ben Zvi 1996c: 137). The Minor Prophets possess their own unique style, theology and structure that sets them apart from one another. The 'book of the Twelve', on the other hand, has none of those features. Apart from a broad chronological development it has no discernible structure. In fact, in the different textual traditions the order of some of the books varies. The Twelve also possess no common theme (Renz 2018; Hadjiev 2020). Even the 'Day of the Lord' motif, which occurs more frequently in the Minor Prophets than anywhere else in the Hebrew Bible, is not pervasive and uniform enough to qualify as an unifying theme for the Twelve (Beck 2005). It features prominently in some scrolls (Joel, Obadiah, Zephaniah) but plays only a marginal, or non-existent, role in others (Hosea, Nahum, Habakkuk, Jonah).

Conclusion

The old position, that the Minor Prophets were originally independent writings and are, at least in the first instance, to be approached as such, has still a lot to commend it. This is not to say that the 'Twelve' cannot, or should not, be read as a collection. However, it has to be clear that such readings are based on the decision of the reader to place the prophetic scrolls in a larger literary, or canonical, context, not the intention of the editors who produced the 'Twelve'. Within such contexts the prophetic books may acquire new meanings, but that still does not negate the necessity of looking at them first and foremost as independent works.

Further study

On the book of the Twelve hypothesis see Nogalski, 1993a,b; Dicou 1994; Jones 1995; Bosshard-Nepustil 1997; Schart 1998; Wöhrle 2006, 2008a. On Joel and the Twelve see Nogalski 2000; Sweeney 2003b; Wöhrle 2010; Jeremias 2012; Troxel 2015b. On Habakkuk and the Twelve see Everson 2003 and Renz 2018. On the Day of the Lord see Beck 2005. More general criticisms of the hypothesis are offered by Ben Zvi 1996c, 2009b; Hadjiev 2009, 2010, 2020. On the Twelve as an anthology see Beck 2006. For a helpful survey of recent scholarship on the Twelve see Jones 2016.

Part One

Joel

---

2   Reading Joel as a composite literary
    work: The structure and unity of the book

3   The contexts of Joel: Historical,
    literary and canonical

4   The setting and genre of Joel

5   Locusts, armies and the Day of the
    Lord in the book of Joel

2

Reading Joel as a composite literary work: The structure and unity of the book

Chapter Outline

The structures of Joel   13
Unity   15
Conclusion: Reading Joel as a composite unity   16
Further study   17

The structures of Joel

The prophecy of Joel begins with calls to lament because devastating natural disasters have befallen the country (1.1–2.11). It culminates with a challenge to the community to return to Yahweh and seek his help (2.12-17). Yahweh responds to this by averting the danger and restoring prosperity (2.18-27). The reader then is given a glimpse of events taking place in the more distant future when the foreign nations, threatening the people of Judah, are defeated and a new world order is established, with Zion at its centre (2.28–3.21).

Interpreters have different opinions on what the macro structure of the book should look like. Some think its two main building blocks are 1.1–2.27 and 2.28–3.21 (Dahmen 2001: 22-7; Jeremias 2007), while others prefer to see a major break coming after 2.17, and not after 2.27 (Strazicich 2007: 40-7; Assis 2013: 53). This is because scholars use different criteria to delineate the text's structure. Some choose to be guided by content, others by formal characteristics. Indeed, formally 1.2–2.17 are presented as the words of the prophet and 2.18–3.21 are divine speech. The distinction is not absolute. Occasionally Yahweh speaks in the first half (1.6-7; 2.12b-13a) and the prophet speaks in the second (2.21-23; 3.11b, 3.16), but those exceptions are not sufficient to alter the overall impression. On the whole, Joel is presented as a human–divine dialogue. In the context of a disaster the people are summoned to cry out to Yahweh in the first half and Yahweh responds to them in the second.

Thematically, however, things look different. The whole of 1.2–2.27 deals primarily with fertility, agriculture, natural disasters and economic hardship. Chapter three, on the other hand, focuses on Israel and the nations and has a more apocalyptic feel about it; that is, it exhibits some similarities to later literature which contains revelations of heavenly mysteries and eschatological events often couched in mythological imagery. The intervening passage, 2.28-32, does not explicitly mention the nations, but it is clearly placed in the same chronological period as the following verses (see 3.1). The portents in heaven and the deliverance in Zion prepare the reader for what follows in 3.9-17. Again, the distinction is not absolute. The motif of enemy nations is present in a metaphorical, or literal, way already in the first part (1.6; 2.1-11, 17, 20, 25), and agricultural images and the theme of fertility resurface in 3.13 and 18, but those are not enough to alter the overall focus of their respective contexts.

The book, therefore, can be read in two different ways. First, as a human–divine dialogue:

Part I: A call to lamentation (1.2–2.17)

> First call to lamentation: Locusts (1.2-20)
> Second call to lamentation: Attacking army (2.1-17)

Part II: Yahweh's response to the people's lamentation (2.18–3.21)

> First response: Restoration of prosperity (2.18-27)
> Second response: Salvation from the nations (2.28–3.21)

Second, Joel can also be approached as a compilation of images of the Day of the Lord:

Part I: The Day of the Lord as an imminent threat (1.2–2.27)

> First description: The Day of the Lord as a locust plague (1.2-12)
> Second description: The Day of the Lord as a drought (1.13-20)
> Third description: The Day of the Lord as an army attack (2.1-11)
> The people's response to the Day of the Lord (2.11-17)
> The Lord's response to the people (2.18-27)

Part II: The Day of the Lord as an eschatological event (2.28–3.21)

> Salvation for those who call on the name of Yahweh (2.28-32)
> Judgement of the nations in the valley of Jehoshaphat (3.1-3)
>> Interlude: judgement on Phoenicia and Philistia (3.4-8)
> Judgement of the nations in the valley of Jehoshaphat continued (3.9-15)
> The transformation and security of Zion (3.16-18)
> Judgement of the nations and the security of Judah (3.19-21)

Unity

There are two different positions in modern scholarship on the unity of Joel. A number of scholars see the material from the second half of the book as a later addition (Barton 2001: 13–14; Roth 2005: 99–109; Jeremias 2007: 3–4; Müller 2008: 19–21). The reasons for this are thematic and literary. The first half of the book (1.2–2.27) is a coherent literary work with its own structure, logic and theme. It envisages a situation of natural disaster in which a cultic prophet issues a call to lamentation, followed by the assurance that Yahweh will respond and replace the disaster with blessing. The second half (2.28–3.21) has a different feel to it. It lacks the tight logic and progression of 1.2–2.27 and gives the impression of being a much looser collection of disparate elements introduced by the phrase 'and then afterwards' (2.28).

Moreover, the chronological and thematic perspectives of the two sections are quite different. In chapters one and two we are still in the realm of history and the Day of the Lord is manifested in natural calamities. In chapter three the Day of the Lord is a unique, final, end-time event focused on the relationship of Israel with the foreign nations, and involving the transformation of Jerusalem and the natural world. The natural disasters of the first two chapters are no longer in view when we come to the second half. In place of the rare and generalized references to the 'nations' we have the names of specific adversaries: the Philistines, the Phoenicians, the Greeks, Edom, Egypt. While in 1.2–2.27 we are moving in the realm of the cult, in 2.28–3.21 we are in the world of the early apocalyptic.

The majority of modern interpreters, however, see the book as a unified literary work, which cannot be understood properly unless its constituent parts are read together (Wolff 1977; Bergler 1988; Hubbard 1989: 31–4; Cook 1995; Strazicich 2007; Assis 2013; Barker 2014). They point to the number of literary and thematic interconnections between the two halves of the book (Assis 2013: 24–30). Many words and phrases from 2.28 to 3.21 point back to the first two chapters, for example,

- 3.15 is a verbatim repetition of 2.10;
- the Day of the Lord is said both to be *near* (1.15–3.14) and to be *great and terrible* (2.11-31);
- *you shall know I am the Lord your God* (2.27–3.17).

This verbal repetition is not arbitrary, but supports deeper thematic connections. In some cases it underlines the theme of reversal in the fortunes of Israel (3.1). The cutting off of *sweet wine* that in 1.5 opens up the description of the calamity is matched by the *sweet wine* that flows from the mountains in 3.18 and symbolizes the new era of prosperity and plenty. Likewise, the dried *watercourses* of 1.20 make the image of *watercourses* overflowing with water in 3.18 all the more powerful.

In other instances the repetition underscores the paradoxical combination of continuity and contrast between the Day of the Lord in chapters one and two and the Day of the Lord in chapter three. The call to Judah to *consecrate* a fast (1.14) and *consecrate* an assembly (2.16) so as to avoid the disaster is matched by a call to the nations to *consecrate* war against Yahweh and his people which will lead to their undoing. The *soldiers and warriors* assembled in that instance (3.9) remind ironically one of the same *soldiers* and *warriors* who in 2.7 were not the object but the instrument of Yahweh's wrath. These examples show that the distinctiveness of theme and literary method in the second part of the book coexists with a dense network of literary allusions that seem like a deliberate attempt to link the material together into a single whole.

The overall structure of the book is also seen as pointing to its unity. Bergler (1988: 69–109) argues that the two disasters (drought in 1.5-13 and enemy attack in 2.1-11) followed by two calls (1.14 and 2.15-17a) and two prayers (1.15-20 and 2.17b) are matched by two divine oracles, the first one related to the drought (2.19-27) and the second related to the enemy attack (2.28–3.21). This outline consciously follows liturgical models which Joel sought to imitate.

Conclusion: Reading Joel as a composite unity

According to Barton (2001: 14), 'We have essentially two separate booklets here, and … they cannot be regarded as forming an organic unity, only an imposed one. … We might nevertheless choose to read Joel as a unity; but it seems clear that this is not a choice that the book itself forces on us, since it gives ample evidence of being a composite work.' Given the numerous thematic and linguistic connections within the book, this judgement goes a bit too far. Such connections invite us to read the book as a whole and see the first half in light of the second. However, they are not enough to demonstrate that Joel forms an organic unity. The links do not obliterate the very different character of the two main sections. All they prove is that the later redactor(s) who added the material in 2.28–3.21 made conscious, intelligent efforts to integrate it well with the work they were editing. Roth (2005: 72) plausibly suggests that the additions come from a period when the issue of Judah and the nations was paramount. The aim of these supplements was to provide Joel with a new relevance in that situation. Therefore, ultimately Barton is on the right track. The unity of the book exists, but it is an imposed one.

This conclusion has implications for the way we read Joel. On the one hand, we can adopt a final-form approach and deal with the text as we now have it. This operation takes its cue from the work of the redactors responsible for the final stages of the book and results in more eschatologically oriented readings. Under the influence of the final chapter even the locust plague at the start is likely to be perceived as somehow pointing towards the final Day of the Lord. On the other hand, we can ignore those final editorial stages and focus our attention entirely on the earlier version of Joel which can still be perceived in 1.1–2.27. This text deals more with the here and now and addresses military disasters and/or natural calamities that take place in the course of history.

The main point is that the redactional history of the text gives readers different options. It allows them to construct different theologies by narrowing or broadening the scope of the work they interpret. Actualizing the prophecy in new circumstances was the main driver of redactional work. A modern reader who is sensitive to the historical depth of the text can benefit from that process of actualization by matching their own context to the relevant stage in the development of the book of Joel.

Further study

For survey of proposals on the structure of Joel see Crenshaw 1995: 29–34. Contrast Dahmen 2001: 22–7 and Jeremias 2007 with Strazicich 2007 and

Assis 2013; also compare the different approaches of Prinsloo 1992 and Garrett 1997: 301–5.

For a survey of scholarship on the unity of Joel see Mason 1994: 103–11 and Barton 2001: 5–14. On the composite nature of Joel, in addition to Barton, see also Redditt 1986; Roth 2005: 99–109; Jeremias 2007: 3–4; Müller 2008: 19–21. Assis 2013: 24–30 and Cook 1995: 181–8 argue for unity. Important earlier works that accepted the unity of the book include Wolff 1977 and Bergler 1988. More recently unity is assumed by Strazicich 2007; Barker 2014.

3

The contexts of Joel: Historical, literary and canonical

Chapter Outline

The historical context of Joel	19
The literary and canonical context: Joel and the book of the Twelve	21
Conclusion: The contexts of Joel	22
Further study	23

The historical context of Joel

According to Assis (2013: 3), 'In order to understand the words of the prophets fully, we must understand their historical background.' Moreover, 'in the absence of an accurate historical context, scholars are unable to interpret the message of Joel correctly' (Assis 2013: 49).

A minority view places Joel in the pre-exilic period, most often towards the end of the monarchy. Garrett (1997: 294) favours a seventh-century date, Stuart (1987: 224–6) a time during the invasions of 701, 598 or 588 BCE and Sweeney (2000a: 150) reads the reference to Egypt in 3.19 against the background of the reign of Josiah. Rudolph (1971: 24–8) suggests a date between 597 and 587 BCE. The most important argument in support of that proposal is that the destruction of the Jerusalem Temple is not explicitly mentioned in Joel and so the exile of 3.1-3 must be a reference to the deportations after the capture of the city in 597 BCE. How much such an argument from silence can carry weight is open to question.

Recently Assis (2013: 3–20) has proposed an exilic date (587–538 BCE). The most obvious difficulty with such a thesis is that the Jerusalem Temple, which plays a central role in the prophecy, was in ruins during that time. Assis addresses the problem by stating that 'the habit of calling a place by a certain name is not easily changed, even when there are substantial changes in the character of the place' (2013: 9). Crucially he points out that in Ezra 3.8 and 5.8 the temple site is termed 'house of God' even before the actual rebuilding of the temple. According to Assis, Joel was speaking into a situation of despair. The people who remained in Judah felt that they had been abandoned by God. They believed that the Day of the Lord, fulfilled in the destruction of Jerusalem, had put an end to their relationship with God (2013: 108). The prophet is trying to convince his audience that, in spite of the disaster, God has not forsaken them, and they should continue to pray and worship at the ruined temple's site.

This proposal is in danger of circularity. It posits that to understand the prophetic words fully we must read them against their historical background, but then uses a particular interpretation of that same prophetic word to determine the precise historical background. On the basis of the reconstructed context Assis postulates, without much evidence, a reluctance on the part of Joel's original audience to engage in cultic action, which then the prophet is said to counter with his preaching. If the aim was to persuade the people to continue to use the site of the ruined temple, it is difficult to understand why this is not expressed more clearly and, instead, the impression of a fully functioning temple cult is created. Assis (2013: 49–50) sees this as part of the rhetorical strategy of the book designed to combat the particular psychological state of the exilic community. The prophet begins with a more immediate problem, the locusts, and sneaks in the topic of the political plight of the people, as it were, through the back door, leading them gradually to a call to resume their contact with God. This is unconvincing. If the people believed to be cut off from God why would they heed the calls in chapter one to lament and gather in sacred assemblies and why would this chapter seek to create the impression that worship at the temple is affected by economic hardship rather than by its destruction and God's withdrawal?

There is a wide agreement that Joel belongs to the Persian period, although scholars differ on whether the book should be placed in the late sixth/fifth century BCE (Ahlström 1971: 111–29; Allen 1976: 19–25; Simkins 1991: 227–8; Crenshaw 1995: 21–9), or in the early part of the fourth century BCE

(Bewer 1911: 56–62; Wolff 1977: 4–6; Barton 2001: 17–18; Jeremias 2007: 2; Nogalski 2011: 202). Four types of arguments are usually employed to arrive at this conclusion.

1. The historical allusions presuppose a later period. The reference to Israel being 'scattered … among the nations' (3.2) and the promise that 'strangers shall never pass again through' Jerusalem (3.17), which presupposes a past or present foreign occupation of the city, are most naturally seen as references to the events of 587 BCE. Since the existence of the temple is presupposed (1.9, 14, 16; 2.17), the book must be written after its rebuilding in 515 BCE. The reference to Jerusalem's walls in 2.7, 9 is seen by some as a pointer to a time after Nehemiah rebuilt them in 445 BCE. According to Wolff (1977: 77–8), 3.4-8 fixes the date in the first half of the fourth century because the text assumes a close political association between Tyre, Sidon and the Philistines which existed only in the fourth century and ended in 343 BCE with the destruction of Sidon. On the other hand, the reference to the Sabeans in 3.8 is thought by many to fit better with the end of the sixth century when these people were still in control of the north Arabian trade routes. Williamson (1982: 1078) regards this argument as questionable since the Sabatea kingdom flourished long after that date.
2. The internal situation of the community reflects the post-exilic period. The community addressed is small enough to gather at the temple. It is ruled by priests and elders. No king is mentioned. The 'grain and drink offering' (1.9, 13; 2.17) presupposes post-exilic cultic practice.
3. It is universally recognized that Joel contains many allusions to and quotations from other biblical texts. These will be explored in more detail in the following chapter. If Joel is dependent on other scripts, this will have to push the date of its composition to the post-exilic period.
4. The language of Joel is thought to be late (see Wolff 1977: 5 and Crenshaw 1995: 26 for details).

The literary and canonical context: Joel and the book of the Twelve

None of these arguments are in and of themselves very strong. Rudolph (1971: 24–8, 45) and Garrett (1997: 286–94) provide a number of good criticisms of all the individual points mentioned earlier. Therefore some scholars remain sceptical about our ability to pinpoint the time of the composition (Mason 1994: 113–16; Prinsloo 1985: 9). But what then is the alternative? Barker (2014) proposes a rhetorical approach which gives up all attempts to look for an identifiable historical setting and instead works with a rhetorical situation that is constructed solely within the 'world of the text' (2014: 39–51). It is, however, doubtful whether such a fictional literary construction is better than historical investigation which can at least rely on some external controls.

Seitz manages to convert our ignorance about the historical context of Joel into a hermeneutical virtue. According to him, our inability to date the text is the key that needs to guide interpretation. Joel is framed on purpose as a timeless message, not as a message addressing a specific situation. The only proper context for it is the canonical one. There was no original audience in the sense in which there was for other prophetic books. The text was part of the book of the Twelve from the start. The general nature of the judgement portrayed in it sums up and anticipates all the judgements to follow in the Twelve (Seitz 2016: 50–64, 113–14). This idea that Joel was composed for its current literary context in the Twelve (Schneider 1979: 80–9) has gained wide currency in recent decades (Nogalski 1993b: 275–8; 2000; Wöhrle 2006: 436–60). However, such a theory rests on a flimsy foundation. As I have argued elsewhere, Joel possesses a distinctiveness which is best explained by its evolution as an independent scroll. Literary links to other Minor Prophets do not suggest that it was written with those prophetic texts in mind (Hadjiev 2020).

Conclusion: The contexts of Joel

The cumulative force of the arguments in favour of a post-exilic setting and the lack of any other credible alternatives make the Persian period as the most likely time for the composition of Joel. This is especially true for the additions in 2.28–3.21 where all of the identifiable historical allusions are located. The original booklet (1.1–2.27) is very general and could theoretically come from the monarchic period, although even there post-exilic era makes more sense.

Further study

For a discussion of the date and a survey of arguments for the Persian period see Allen 1976: 19–25, Wolff 1977: 4–6 and Crenshaw 1995: 21–9. A criticism of those arguments and a suggestion for a pre-exilic date can be found in Rudolph 1971: 24–8 and Garrett 1997: 286–94. Ahlström 1971: 1–22 investigates the language of Joel and dates it to the late pre-exilic/early post-exilic period. For an exilic date see Assis 2013. Consult also the survey and discussion of Williamson 1982: 1077–8 and Mason 1994: 113–16 according to whom the date 'remains a mystery'.

Barker 2014 proposes a rhetorical, final-form approach and Seitz 2016 argues for the canonical setting as the proper context of the book. For Joel in the book of the Twelve see also the more historically oriented work of Nogalski 1993b; Bosshard-Nepustil 1997: 269–97; Wöhrle 2006: 436–60. For a criticism of this position see Hadjiev 2020.

4

The setting and genre of Joel

Chapter Outline

A cultic book?	24
An apocalyptic book?	25
A 'learned prophecy'?	27
Two didactic books about the present and the future	29
Further study	30

A cultic book?

Joel's language and thought betray a close proximity to the temple cult. This is evident in his concern that the natural disaster has affected temple worship, in his focus on priests, offerings and temple assemblies and in the call to perform cultic actions like fasting, weeping and lamentation. The influence of Zion theology can be discerned in Jerusalem's description as a holy mountain, a divine dwelling and a place of refuge, as well as in the topos of the nations' attack on the city and the life-giving river flowing out of it. The structure of the prophecy reflects the cultic pattern of a lamentation liturgy: a communal lament followed by divine oracles of assurance (Bergler 1988: 111–30).

On this basis many scholars assume that Joel was a cultic prophet who functioned in the temple (Kapelrud 1948: 176–7; Ahlström 1971: 136–7; Hubbard 1989: 27–8; Strazicich 2007: 50–1; Hagedorn 2011a: 234 n. 36). Some even understand the book as the text of a national lament liturgy (Watts 1975: 12–13; Blenkinsopp 1996: 224), performed as a response to either a severe locust plague (so Cook 1995: 180–1, 188–94) or military defeats (so Ogden 1983, 1987). Others, however, see here only an imitation of cultic language and forms. Wolff (1977: 9–10) argues that the text bears the marks of literary embellishment which suggests that it stands at some distance from an actual liturgical performance. Bellinger (1984: 86–9) reaches the same conclusion because, in his view, Joel address a specific historical situation and does not portray a recurring cultic event.

Barton (2001: 21–2) strikes a middle course. On the one hand, he agrees with Wolff that Joel's language draws on liturgical forms, but does not directly stem from temple worship. On the other, he interprets the main point of the prophecy as calling the people to convene an actual cultic assembly in response to disasters that were happening, a call appropriate to cultic prophets or even perhaps priests.

An apocalyptic book?

Joel has also some affinities to later apocalyptic literature. These include the anticipation of a final battle between God and his enemies (3.9-16) followed by a new state of security and prosperity for his people (3.16-21), and the use of mythical paradigms: the extravagant fertility, a fountain flowing from the temple (3.18), the shaking of the earth and the darkening of the skies (2.30; 3.15-16). The outpouring of the divine spirit which results in prophecies, dreams and visions (2.28-29) may have some connections to later apocalyptic obsession with revelation of heavenly secrets via supernatural means.

An influential attempt to link these early apocalyptic traits in Joel to a possible sociological context comes from Plöger (1968: 106–17). He hypothesized a growing division within the post-exilic community around the issues of eschatology which also left its mark on the text of Joel (1968: 96–105). The first part of the book is an embellished literary record of a real-life event in which a natural disaster was overcome by cultic means. It uses the Day of the Lord concept of earlier prophecy in a 'metaphorical-liturgical' sense to describe the locust plague. The additions of chapter three reassert an eschatological interpretation of the Day by portraying it as a future event that will separate Israel and the nations (1968: 98–101). The last addition (2.28-32) takes this a step further. There appears now an internal, albeit hidden, division within Israel marked by the outpouring of the Spirit. Only the true Israel will be saved, and the true Israel is defined as the Israel who 'has responded to the eschatological faith and considers the day of Yahweh as an eschatological reality' (1968: 103). Plöger postulates the origins of apocalyptic thought in anti-establishment circles and thus places the redaction of Joel in peripheral groups existing at the fringes of the community living in the Persian province of Judah (Yehud).

This approach has been very influential (Petersen 1977; Wilson 1980: 290). Redditt (1986) has developed it further, postulating that the first half of Joel be ascribed to an establishment group, while the second part stems from peripheral prophets opposed to the establishment. According to Roth (2005: 107–9) the authors of chapter three still belonged to the scribal establishment of Jerusalem. It is only with the last addition to the book (2.28-32) from the Hellenistic period that the contours of a sectarian, apocalyptic group can be perceived. Those who see Joel as a unified composition think that the book as a whole is an implied polemic against the ideology and central institutions, most notably the cult, of post-exilic Yehud (Wolff 1977: 10–2; see also Coggins 2000: 20–4).

However, such a thesis is not without its problems. Cook (1995) argues against the theory that apocalyptic thinking is necessarily caused by deprivation, and to be always associated with marginal groups. He has shown that millennial groups with alive eschatological expectations can be found close to the power centres of their respective societies. In the book of Joel cultic and apocalyptic features are closely intertwined, suggesting that the book as a whole originates with a priestly group from the Zadokite branch that was part of Jerusalem's central temple structures. The group saw the locust plague as a harbinger of apocalyptic events and sought to mobilize the whole community to engage in a cultic response which might avert the looming apocalyptic disaster.

While Cook overstates the case for an essential unity of Joel, his point that there is no explicit indication of inner-community strife in the text of the prophecy has considerable merit (Cook 1995: 206–9). The tension in the final chapter is not between different social and religious groups within Israel but between Israel and the nations. Therefore, even if Joel's initial text received proto-apocalyptic additions in 2.28–3.21, there is no reason to think that the people responsible for its transmission and redaction came from a different social setting. Esler (2014) argues that in apocalyptic literature one often finds not so much resistance to imperial domination, but ethnic conflict and attempts to preserve ethnic identity over against other groups. Joel fits much more naturally into such an interpretative framework. It is more easily read as a scribal attempt to provide a vision of the future that serves to preserve and enhance the community's identity against the surrounding hostile peoples, than as the literature of a peripheral, disenfranchised group fighting against the establishment.

A 'learned prophecy'?

Another striking feature of Joel is the vast number of verbal and thematic connections to other parts of the Hebrew Bible. For a list of fourteen widely agreed cases of literary citations in Joel see Williamson (1982: 1078). There are several textual complexes that seem to be particularly important to the authors of the book. The locust infestation (1.4; 2.25) reminds one of the eighth Egyptian plague from the Exodus narrative. The emphasis on the incomparability of the disaster (Joel 1.2–Exod. 10.6, 14), the exhortation to tell future generations about it (Joel 1.3–Exod. 10.2) and the recognition formula (Joel 2.27–Exod. 8.18, 10.2) strengthen further the connection between these texts.

Isaiah 13.2-16 stands in the background of Joel 1.5–2.11. Joel 1.15 looks like a direct quote from Isa. 13.6, and the 'wail' of Isa. 13.6 plays a key structuring role in Joel 1.5-13. There are also a number of correspondences between the pictures of an advancing army in Joel 2.1-11 and Isaiah 13: great army on the mountains (Joel 2.2–Isa. 13.4) causing fear and dismay (Joel 2.6a–Isa. 13.8a), plundering the houses (Joel 2.9–Isa. 13.16), making the earth desolate (Joel 2.3–Isa. 13.5, 9) and culminating in the darkening of the luminaries and the shaking of heaven and earth (Joel 2.10–Isa. 13.10, 13). Jeremias (2000) suggests that the two calamities in Joel are in fact patterned on the two mentions of the Day of the Lord in Isaiah 13 (Isa. 13.6–Joel 1.15 and Isa. 13.9–Joel 2.1).

A number of other prophetic traditions have close parallels to Joel. The second half of the book contains several literary links to Obadiah: 'In Mount Zion and in Jerusalem there shall be those who escape, as the Lord has said' (Joel 2.32–Obadiah 17); 'they cast lots for my people' (Joel 3.3–Obadiah 11); 'I will turn your deeds back upon your heads' (Joel 3.4, 7–Obadiah 15). The book culminates with the mention of Edom, the main focus of Obadiah's prophecy, as one of the two enemy nations symbolizing Judah's oppressors (Joel 3.19). The 'northerner' in Joel 2.20 recalls the 'foe from the north' of Jeremiah 4–6 and Ezekiel 38–39, the fountain from the temple (Joel 3.18) corresponds to the picture in Ezek. 47.1-12, while the nations' attack on Jerusalem followed by their defeat, the outpouring of the divine spirit and the sanctification of Zion parallel Zechariah 9–14 (Mason 1994: 120).

Most scholars explain these connections with the hypothesis that Joel was a student of written texts, a 'learned prophet' (Wolff 1977: 10–12) who interpreted, applied and actualized these texts for his own time (Bergler

1988: 344). The proponents of the 'book of the Twelve' hypothesis argue that the primary function of the quotations in Joel was to tie it more closely to the wider context of the Twelve. For example, Joel 3.16, 18 links the text with Amos 1.2 and 9.13, while Joel 3.10 with Mic. 4.3. According to Müller (2008) Joel is a multidimensional text that can be read on two different planes. The first consists of the text of Joel taken on its own. The multiple connections to earlier traditions point to a second plane, a cluster of themes and ideas that is constantly present in the background and opens up a deeper dimension of meaning. Joel's theology of the Day of the Lord can be fully grasped only when this deeper dimension is taken into consideration.

Strazicich (2007) offers a reading, based on the premise that the book appropriates and resignifies earlier texts. Joel's use of these texts is supported by two different types of hermeneutics. First, a hermeneutic of prophetic critique transforms traditions about Yahweh's actions against foreign nations into a depiction of judgement on his people. Judah takes the place of Egypt as the victim of a new exodus-type locust plague (1.4) and the place of Babylon (Isa. 13) and Egypt (Ezek. 30) as the object of a new Day of the Lord enemy attack (1.15; 2.1-11). In 2.12-14 the appropriation of Jon. 3.9 and 4.2 serves to underline a message of hope. If Yahweh was willing to pardon the Assyrians, he will surely be merciful to his own repentant people. This sets the scene for the second part of the book where a 'hermeneutic of constituency' adapts and actualizes various texts to paint the picture an eschatological-apocalyptic Day of the Lord that will bring about the restoration of Zion.

Not everybody, however, would agree with such an approach. Some think that Joel is dependent on traditional lore perhaps transmitted orally in connection with the cult or simply uses common stock phrases (Ahlström 1971: 72–97; Rudolph 1971: 26–7; Simkins 1991: 266–73). For example, the call 'beat your ploughshares into swords and your pruning hooks into spears' (Joel 3.10) sounds like a proverbial, or a cultic (Coggins 1982: 89), expression that appears independently in Mic. 4.3 = Isa. 2.4. The different Hebrew terms for 'spear' ($r^e m\bar{a}h\hat{i}m$ in Joel and $h\breve{a}n\hat{i}\underline{t}\hat{o}\underline{t}$ in Micah and Isaiah) are the kind of variation one would expect from oral tradition (Simkins 1991: 235). Moreover, reading Joel with Micah and Isaiah in mind here does little to enhance our understanding of the text. The same can be argued about the 'Amos quotations' in Joel 3.16, 18 (Ahlström 1971: 87–8; Coggins 1982: 90), or the links with Isaiah 13 (Culley 2000: 57–60). Barton points out that a lot of the 'quotations' in Joel are well-known liturgical formulas. He postulates the wide circulation of anonymous, 'free-floating' oracles that were utilized independently in various prophetic scripts (Barton 2001: 24–6, 153).

Two didactic books about the present and the future

Whether Joel is a literary composition which consistently interprets earlier texts or a work utilizing the imagery and language of widespread oral traditions, its didactic intention is unmistakable (Roth 2005: 58; Jeremias 2007: 11–2). According to Limburg (1988: 56), 'Behind the book of Joel is a story about a crisis and a deliverance from that crisis. That story has been shaped into something of a liturgy so that future generations can hear the story once again and also discover what to do in their own times of crisis.' This approach has been developed in some detail by Troxel (2015a). According to him the first two chapters of the book are a didactic narrative. The story to be told is introduced with the 'call to receive instruction' in 1.2-3 and consists of two parts: a crisis (1.4–2.17) and a deliverance (2.19b-27). The passage in 2.18-19a, with its verbs in the past tense, is part of the narrator's report that marks the transition between the two main sections. The deliverance is recounted in order to teach future generations how to respond to the impending threat of the Day of the Lord (2.28-32) by imitating the return of their forebears (2.12-17).

Troxel's proposal leaves open the question how the additions in chapter three impact the didactic thrust of the text. These additions maintain the scribal interest of the first section as they seek to reapply the teaching of the book to new situations. We can, in fact, talk about two different didactic texts simultaneously present in Joel. The first one focuses heavily on the cult and may have had its original provenance there (1.1–2.27). It teaches the worshipping community how to respond with cultic means to various crises that may come its way and threaten its existence. The second text is a proto-apocalyptic reworking of the first and includes the whole of the present book of Joel. The additions suggest a situation in which the community was under threat because of the pressure exerted on it by various neighbouring groups. To counter such pressure Joel constructs and defends the identity of the community by looking first at the past and then at the future. The past defines this community as a nation which has experienced Yahweh's delivering power in the context of military attacks and natural disasters (1.1–2.27). The future confirms such an identity with a vision of a final and decisive intervention of Yahweh on its behalf (2.28–3.21).

The two texts teach different lessons to their respective audiences. The first assumes the possibility of change in history. It invites the reader in times of scarcity and famine to turn to Yahweh who can overcome all present difficulties and bring prosperity. The second text pushes salvation from current difficulties into the eschatological future. It exhorts its audience to have an attitude of quiet trust and orient all its expectations towards the time when Yahweh will repeat on an universal scale his mighty acts of judgement and salvation.

Further study

For Joel's relationship to the cult consult Kapelrud 1948; Ahlström 1971; Ogden 1983, 1987; Blenkinsopp 1996; Cook 1995 and contrast Wolff 1977 and Bellinger 1984.

On the genre of apocalyptic literature see Collins 1979, 2014. On prophecy and apocalyptism see Collins 2015: 54–69 and the literature cited there. On the connection of Joel's apocalyptic sections with peripheral groups see Plöger 1968 and Redditt 1986. For an argument that places the origin of Joel's proto-apocalyptic thought within the priestly establishment see Cook 1995. More generally on apocalyptism's link with priestly and scribal establishment groups see Cook 2014; Davies 1989.

On Joel as learned prophecy and its use of earlier traditions see Bergler 1988; Strazicich 2007; Müller 2008 and contrast Simkins 1991 and Barton 2001. On Joel's use of traditional language see also Culley 2000 and Coggins 1982. For the proposal to read the book as a didactic narrative see Troxel 2015a.

5

Locusts, armies and the Day of the Lord in the book of Joel

Chapter Outline

The disaster	31
The Day of the Lord	34
Conclusion: The Day of the Lord in the two books of Joel	36
Further study	37

The reader of Joel is faced with two major interpretative problems. In chapters one and two the book depicts a disaster that threatens the community. But what precisely is this disaster? In two key sections the prophet talks about a locust infestation (1.4; 2.25). The language of scorched earth, shrivelled seeds of grain and dried up water courses in 1.17-20 and the promise of rain in 2.23-24, however, is more appropriate to a description of a drought. On top of all this, in 2.1-11 the image of an invading army dominates the scene (see also 1.6 and 2.20). The second interpretative problem is that the disaster is somehow linked to an expectation of the coming Day of the Lord, an expression that appears with relative frequency in Joel and spans the whole book (1.15; 2.1, 11, 31; 3.14). But what exactly is this Day of the Lord and how is it related to the disaster?

The disaster

Scholars have answered the question about the nature of the disaster in a number of different ways.

(1) *Chapters one and two refer to a literal locust plague.* The locusts in 1.6 and the invader in 2.4-9 are compared to an army. Since to compare soldiers to an army is nonsensical the most logical solution is that the army in 2.1-11 is a metaphor for the locusts. Its description (2.4-9) contains a number of elements appropriate to an advancing locust swarm, for example, jumping through the windows. Simkins (1991: 121–69) suggests that chapter one describes the impact of a locust plague in the spring of the preceding year, compounded by the effects of the dry Palestinian summer. Chapter two then refers to a subsequent infestation in the following year. Barton (2001: 44–8, 68–70) thinks the two chapters are parallel descriptions of a single event (cf. Prinsloo 1985: 47; Hubbard 1989: 53 n. 1).

(2) *Chapters one and two refer to military invasions.* Andiñach (1992) argues that the locusts should not be interpreted literally but taken as a metaphor for a human army. Stuart (1987: 226, 232–4, 241–2) suggests that they are an anticipation of the Babylonian, or Assyrian, invasion. Ogden (1983: 104–5, 1987) thinks in terms of four different attacks from various foreign powers, which took place around the destruction of Jerusalem in 587 BCE. The images of locusts, fire and drought were images used in the liturgy of lament to portray the devastation caused by the attacks.

(3) *The locusts imagery operates simultaneously on two levels: a literal and a metaphorical* (Assis 2013: 39–41). Joel is speaking about a real locust infestation, but at the same time uses it to depict symbolically the Babylonian invasion (on the reasons for this, see Chapter 3, p. 20). The same dynamic can be perceived in the second half of the book. The agricultural imagery is utilized in the depiction of political deliverance (3.13, 18) and the reversal of the agricultural disaster includes references to the nations (2.17) and the defeat of the 'northerner' (2.20). At a deeper level the national deliverance in the second part of the book is presented as an answer to the problems of natural disaster in the first.

(4) *Chapter one describes a literal locust plague, chapter two an impending military invasion, which is not seen as an eschatological event.* Beck (2005: 165–7) reads this against the background of the fourth century BCE. Garrett (1997: 298–301, 343), who dates the book to the seventh century BCE, sees in chapter two an anticipation of the Babylonians.

(5) *Chapter one describes a locust invasion; chapter two refers to a future apocalyptic army.* The two events have to be seen as separate and subsequent to one another (Wolff 1977: 41–2). The communal lamentation and the predominance of verbs in the perfect in 1.4-20 suggest that a past occurrence is described in chapter one. The call to alarm and the predominance of imperfect forms in 2.1-11 point to a future event. The possibility of repentance and aversion of the disaster, implied in 2.12-17, distinguishes it from the calamity in 1.4-20 which, one must assume, cannot be averted. The army in 2.1-11 is the mythical enemy from the north described with imagery derived from theophanic traditions, and it is significant that the locusts are not mentioned at all in that passage. The two interrelated deliverances in the second half of Joel correspond to these two threats: a historical deliverance from the natural disaster in 2.18-27 and a future apocalyptic salvation in 2.28–3.21 (Cook 1995: 181–4).

(6) *The fusion of imagery results from the complicated redactional history of the text.* Hagedorn (2011a: 234–66) suggests that an original thanksgiving liturgy about deliverance from a locust plague and a drought was reworked by various additions (1.6-7, 15, 2.1-14). As a result, the locusts were portrayed as an invading army and the natural disaster from which the community was saved by the intervention of Yahweh was reinterpreted as a manifestation and foretaste of the Day of the Lord, imagined in military terms. Wöhrle (2006: 391–435) argues that the first draft of Joel was about a deliverance from a drought, portrayed as the Day of the Lord. A later redaction, concerned with the relationship of Judah to the foreign nations, added the image of an attacking army. In order to better connect that image to the natural disaster that formed the substance of the original text, the redactor portrayed that army metaphorically as locusts.

(7) *The locusts and the military invasion are metaphorical descriptions intended to convey a theological message.* Dahmen (2001: 59) understands 2.1-11 as a literary presentation of typical military disasters, and Deist (1988) argues that that there are no references in Joel to any calamities in the real world; the book is a literary collage of images and metaphors that describe the nature of Day of the Lord. Culley (2000: 60) suggests that the description of disaster in Joel is defined not by the contours of any specific event but by the traditional language and imagery used.

Mason (1994: 102) notes that the general nature of the language may result from the cultic origin and reuse of the text.

According to Bergler (1988: 247–76, 335–42) the real disaster that prompted the composition of Joel was not a locust plague but a drought. Joel combined a pre-existing 'drought poem' (still preserved in parts of 1.5-20) with another pre-existing poem on the 'foe from the north' (now found in 1.6-8 and 2.1-9*), but not because there were two separate threats to the well-being of Judah. He simply wanted to escalate the description of the disaster and followed a common two-step liturgical scheme. Most importantly, the drought was interpreted by him with the help of allusions to the exodus narrative, primarily to the locust plague and to some of the other plagues (see the references to blood and darkness). By such means, Joel depicted the current disaster that his community was facing typologically, as another exodus plague brought about by the Lord. The point of the connection was to understand theologically the present events, reading them in the light of the past actions of God and establishing a connection that would allow the audience to perceive their inner meaning. The drought was a 'locust-plague' sent by Yahweh, and Judah had a choice: perish like Pharaoh or return to God.

The Day of the Lord

References to the Day of the Lord span the book and provide it with its most characteristic, unifying theme. However, the development of this theme is not straightforward. Joel, in fact, offers several different pictures of the Day of the Lord (Deist 1988; Crenshaw 1995: 49–50). According to Rendtorff (2000: 78–80) in chapters one and two the Day of the Lord is a divine threat against Israel that can be averted by turning to God; in 2.28-32 it is a destructive and universal eschatological event that will be escaped only by individuals, Israelites and foreigners alike, who call on the name of the Lord; in chapter three it is a punishment for Israel's enemies. The question is how do these varying concepts of the Day of the Lord relate to each other?

Simkins (1991: 203–79) removes all tension between the different Day of the Lord pictures by arguing that the Day does not entail any divine punishment on Judah even in the first half of the book. He stresses the absence of explicit references to Yahweh's wrath and judgement and interprets both the locusts and the nations not as agents of Yahweh but as his enemies who attack his people, challenge his kingship and threaten cosmic order. The

Day of the Lord, then, is an 'event in the history of creation' in which Yahweh intervenes to fight a cosmogonic battle, defeat his foes, rescue his land and people and renew creation. This approach, however, is dependent on interpreting the locust army of 2.1-9 as distinct from and opposed to Yahweh's army of 2.11, which is not the most natural reading of this text.

Most commentators see the Day of the Lord in chapters one and two as a day of judgement against Judah, the reasons for which are left unspecified (see Crenshaw 1995: 146 for an overview of suggestions). The locust plague was a portent of that Day (Prinsloo 1985: 33, 38). The Day itself, according to Strazicich, was an imminent historical act of judgement, a military invasion, which was averted as the community heeded Joel's call to repent. In 2.28–3.21 the Day of the Lord not only is postponed as a result of the repentance but also reversed into a day of salvation for Judah. It manifests itself as the apocalyptic end of history, which brings justice to Israel and liberation from the oppression of foreign nations (Strazicich 2007: 55–8, 111–12, 118, 166, 175).

In the NT the Day of the Lord is also linked to the eschatological future by the author of the book of Acts (2.17-21) but reinterpreted from a Christian perspective. The text of Joel 2.28-32 is taken to depict the final stages of human history ushered by the cross and the resurrection of Christ. To underline that point Acts 2.17 substitutes the more neutral 'afterwards' of Joel 2.28 with the less ambiguous expression 'in the last days'. The outpouring of the Spirit on 'all flesh' (Joel 2.28) finds its fulfilment in the events on the day of Pentecost (Acts 2.1-4) and marks the beginning of the eschatological process. The Day of the Lord (Acts 2.20) is the great day of judgement and salvation, which arrives after the manifestation of various apocalyptic signs in heaven and on earth, and brings that process to a climax and a conclusion.

These readings presuppose the unity of the book and seek to discover coherence in the overall picture of the Day of the Lord. Things look different if one assumes that Joel is a composite work. The most radical representative of this position is Barton who sees in Joel two quite different and essentially unrelated concepts of the Day. In the first section the natural disasters are interpreted as a manifestation of the Day of the Lord in history. This standpoint is similar to the way the Day appears in Amos – as an occasion of decisive divine judgement on Judah. In the second half of the book there is a completely different version of the Day of the Lord tradition, one more akin to the popular concepts that were current even during the time of Amos and were in fact attacked by him. According to this understanding the Day was a transformation of the world order which would establish the people of Israel at its power centre and bring down their enemies (Barton 2004: 71–3, 2001: 60–2, 70).

A middle of the road position is offered by Müller (2008: 195–210). She also sees different ideas of the Day of the Lord as resulting from redactional interventions but at the same time attempts to see some overall conceptual unity. In the first half of the book the Day of the Lord is not an exclusively past or future event but a present reality from the point of view of the reader/ listener. She understands the focus of attention to be not on the natural and military calamities. These are only images attempting to capture an indescribable theophanic reality. The Day of the Lord is the coming of Yahweh himself. That encounter has the potential to bring both judgement and salvation, but its ultimate aim is for the community to come to the knowledge of Yahweh (2.27). Chapter three and 2.28-32 are two different additions that modify the picture of the Day by restricting it to the future. Zion now is a place of salvation, not a place under threat. The nations have no longer an option to turn to Yahweh in chapter three, while in 2.28-32 salvation is on an individual basis and is connected to the outpouring of the Spirit. These attempts to actualize and narrow the concept of the Day of the Lord result in telescoping the present and the future when the book as a whole is considered. The Day is an eschatological event, which is based in the present where the encounter with divine reality takes place.

Conclusion: The Day of the Lord in the two books of Joel

At the end of last chapter I suggested that in Joel we find two different didactic books: the original composition (1.1–2.27) and the final form achieved by the additions in 2.28–3.21. These two books present the reader with two different concepts of the Day of the Lord. The original booklet describes how past Days of the Lord were survived by the people who turned to Yahweh and experienced his merciful restoration. The language is general enough to apply both to natural calamities and to military disasters and so to teach future generations of readers how to respond to such challenges regardless of the historical particularities of their respective situations. The choice between locusts, military attack or drought therefore may be a false one. The blend of a variety of traditional images serves to facilitate future reapplication whenever the Day of the Lord threatens the community of faith.

The second didactic book is the final form of Joel as we now have it, created by the apocalyptic additions in 2.28–3.21, which redirect the thrust of the original book. These additions transform the concept of the Day of the Lord from a theological tool for understanding the past and copying with the present into an eschatological concept that provides a radical hope relegated to the distant future. The past and current manifestations of the Day are symbols of its ultimate apocalyptic unveiling.

Further study

The locusts are interpreted literally by Simkins 1991 and Barton, 2001, metaphorically as a human army by Andiñach 1992 and as an apocalyptic army in chapter two by Wolff 1977 and Cook 1995. Assis 2013 maintains both the literal and the metaphorical interpretations. Bergler 1988 and Culley 2000 see the images as traditional. A very useful and detailed exploration of the physiology and behaviour of locusts can be found in Simkins 1991: 107–20. For redaction-critical solutions consult Wöhrle 2006 and Hagedorn 2011a.

On the Day of the Lord generally see Van Leeuwen 1974; Everson 1974; Hoffmann 1981. For the Day of the Lord in Joel consult Deist 1988; Simkins 1991; Barton 2004; Strazicich 2007; Müller 2008. Rendtorff 2000 discusses the key role that Joel's Day of the Lord plays in the Twelve.

Part Two

Obadiah

6   The composition and unity of the
    book of Obadiah

7   The historical background of Obadiah

8   The genre, setting and purpose of
    Obadiah

9   Edom and the image of the other

6

The composition and unity of the book of Obadiah

Chapter Outline

Further study   44

The book of Obadiah is an oracle against a single nation – the Edomites – who are condemned in it for their crimes against the people of Judah. It falls into two distinct parts: the first deals with Edom's transgressions and punishment (vv. 1-14) while the second focuses on the deliverance of Zion (vv. 16-21). These two sections are linked by v. 15 which can be taken either as a conclusion to the preceding material (Dicou 1994: 25–7) or as an introduction of the following (Stuart 1987: 414), and so functions as a bridge between them when the text is read synchronically.

There are a number of reasons to think that Obadiah is a composite text. Its opening paragraph has unmistakable literary connections to parts of Jeremiah 49, as can be seen from the table below:

Obadiah	Jeremiah 49
1 *We* have heard a report from the LORD, and a messenger has been sent among the nations:	14 *I* have heard a report from the LORD, and a messenger has been sent among the nations:
'Rise up **and let us rise** against her for battle!'	'**Gather yourselves together and come** against her, and rise up for battle!'
2 Behold I made you small among the nations;	15 **For** behold I made you small among the nations,
you were utterly despised.	despised *by humankind.*

3 The pride of your heart deceived you,
you who live in the clefts of the rock,
on high is *his dwelling*.
You say in your heart,
'Who will bring me down to the ground?'

4 *If* you go high like the eagle,
if **among the stars is set** your nest,
from there I will bring you down,
says the LORD.

5 If thieves **came to you**,
if plunderers by night
– how you have been destroyed!
– would they not steal only what they wanted?

If grape-gatherers came to you, *would* they not leave gleanings?

16a **The terror you inspire** deceived
you, and the pride of your heart,
you who live in the clefts of the rock,
you who hold the height of
the hill.

16b *Although* you make high as the eagle your nest,
from there I will bring you down,
says the LORD.

9 If grape-gatherers came to you,
[would] they not leave gleanings?
If thieves by night,
they would pillage only what they wanted.

Many think that Obadiah adapted the oracle directly from Jeremiah 49 (Nogalski 1993b: 61–8; Dicou 1994: 58–73; Raabe 1996: 22–31; Renkema 2003: 38; Jeremias 2007: 62–5; Hagedorn 2011a: 189), but the types of variations between the two texts make it more likely that both used independently an oracle that came to them from a pool of common tradition (Allen 1976: 132–3; Coggins 1985: 73; Wolff 1986: 38–40; Stuart 1987: 415–16; Mason 1991: 90; Ben Zvi 1996a: 99–114; Barton 2001: 125–6). So rather than being a totally original composition, it is clear that Obadiah used at least some pre-existing materials and gave them a new interpretation and application.

Some interpreters contend that the book is essentially a unified literary work (Allen 1976: 133–6; Renkema 2003: 38–9; Block 2017: 21–46). Raabe (1996: 14–22) argues that it possess a coherence at the structural and literary level and everything in it could reflect the thinking of a single individual, speaking either on a singular occasion or over a more prolonged period of time. Most, however, accept that the text of Obadiah is composite, even though they envisage the precise process of its evolution differently. Here is a sample of some recent reconstructions.

- Obadiah is a mosaic of pre-existing anti-Edom sayings collated and adapted for their use in the book of the Twelve (Nogalski 1993b: 61–92, 276–7; 2011: 368–76).

- Verses 8-18 are a ninth-century oracle against Edom which was reworked during the sixth century BCE with the addition of vv. 1-7 and 19-21 (Sweeney 2000a: 280–5).
- Verses 1-9 were a late pre-exilic prophecy accusing Edom of arrogance. In light of the changing historical situation it was updated twice: (i) after 587 BCE with an oracle (vv. 10-14+15b) accusing Edom of participating in the destruction of Jerusalem; (ii) later on vv. 15a, 16-21 were added, accusing the Edomites of appropriation of Judean land (Assis 2014; 2016: 141–50).
- Verses 1-14, 15b and 15a, 16-21 were two originally independent pieces combined at a later stage (Barton 2001: 118–19).
- Verses 1-14, 15b, 21 were Obadiah's original collection of sayings about Edom. This collection was subsequently supplemented with the addition of two independent words from the prophet from a later period (vv. 15b+16-17 and v. 18) and two even later redactional comments in vv. 19-20 (Wolff 1986: 21–2, 45, 62). With the inevitable variation in detail, a broadly similar approach is adopted by many critics (Bewer 1911: 3–9; Rudolph 1971: 295–8; Dicou 1994: 101–4; Hagedorn 2011a: 186–214).

There are two reasons to separate the first (vv. 1-14) and the second (vv. 16-21) part of the book into different compositional layers: (i) the thematic tensions that exist between them and (ii) the different historical situations presupposed by them (Rudolph 1971: 296; Barton 2001: 118):

1. The role of the nations is different: in vv. 1-14 they are the tool for Edom's punishment; in vv. 16-21 they are the object of judgement.
2. The object of the threat is different: Edom in vv. 1-14, the nations in vv. 15-21.
3. The means of judgement are different: the nations in v. 5, the house of Jacob/Joseph in v. 18.
4. The addressees are different: Edom in vv. 1-15 (second person singular), Judah in v. 16 (second person plural).
5. The focus is different: vv. 1-14 seem to have a specific historical situation in mind, vv. 15-21 are more general, even 'eschatological', with their introduction of the Day of the Lord theme. Related to this final point is the contention that vv. 1-14 and vv. 16-21 reflect two different historical backgrounds. The first part fits with the immediate aftermath of the destruction of Jerusalem in the sixth century BCE, while vv. 16-21 require a later date. This issue will be taken up in the following chapter.

The one verse that does not fit neatly this division is v. 15. Thematically it belongs to the following: it introduces the theme of the Day of the Lord coming against all nations. Formally it looks like a continuation of the preceding: it still addresses Edom and uses the second person singular. Wellhausen (1898: 213) pointed out that, in fact, the second half of the verse fits well immediately after vv. 1-14. So it is possible that v. 15b was the original conclusion of the first part which was separated from it when v. 15a was inserted.

All this is not to deny the literary quality of the finished product. Anderson (2010) explores the considerable literary skill with which the language of Obadiah underlines the parallels between Jacob and Esau and the poetic justice of Edom's punishment which corresponds closely to his crimes. There are also a number of literary features that span the different redactional sections and unify the book. For example the phrase 'mount Esau' (vv. 8, 9, 19, 21) is characteristic of Obadiah and appears nowhere else in the OT. It also plays an important role forming a contrast with 'my holy mountain' (v. 16) and 'mount Zion' (v. 17) and prepares the way for the concluding contrast between the two mountains in v. 21. The tenfold repetition of the word 'day' in vv. 11-14 culminates in the 'day of the Lord' saying of v. 15. Together with the formula in v. 8, this brings the total number of mentions of the word 'day' in Obadiah to twelve. The final 'going up' the mountains in v. 21 contrasts with the theme of Edom's unsuccessful attempts to elevate himself in the beginning of the book and Yahweh's corresponding threat to 'bring him down' (vv. 2-4). This is not enough to prove that the prophecy is composed by a single author, but it shows that the redactors, who supplemented the original booklet in vv. 1-14, 15b with the additions in the later half, made a conscious effort to integrate the different materials into a literary whole.

The book of Obadiah, therefore, exhibits certain similarities to Joel. We have in effect two books before us: an earlier text which deals with a historical crisis (vv. 1-14, 15b) and the final text which introduces an eschatological dimension to this crisis by means of redactional additions.

Further study

On the composition of the book see Rudolph 1971; Wolff 1986; Mason 1991; Raabe 1996; Barton 2001; Assis 2014, 2016. For a discussion of the structure see Allen 1976; Snyman 1989; Renkema 2003; Jenson 2008. On the literary artistry of Obadiah see Anderson 2010. The relationship of Obadiah with Jeremiah 49 is discussed by Wolff 1986; Nogalski 1993b; Dicou 1994; Raabe 1996; Ben Zvi 1996a; Jeremias 2007.

7

The historical background of Obadiah

Chapter Outline

The sin of Edom (vv. 10-14)	45
The punishment of Edom (vv. 7-9)	47
The date(s) of Obadiah	47
Further study	48

The sin of Edom (vv. 10-14)

The reason for Edom's vehement condemnation, according to Obad. 10, is the 'slaughter and violence' committed against the population of Judah (taking with NRSV the last word of v. 9 together with v. 10). This charge is detailed in vv. 12-14. Instead of a straightforward description of Edom's crime there we have a series of prohibitions: 'Do not gloat/rejoice/boast' (ESV). If one takes the prohibitions at face value (as does Niehaus 1993) then the actions of Edom must lie in the present, or in the future. However, most interpreters agree that this is a rhetorical device to depict past actions. Perhaps Obadiah imaginatively places himself in the past in order to enhance the dramatic effect of his words (Jenson 2008: 19). NRSV translates the commands as 'you should not have gloated'.

Obadiah 11 says that the crimes of Edom took place on the day when 'foreigners entered the gates of Jerusalem' and carried off its wealth. This is most likely a reference to the Babylonian sack of Jerusalem in 587 BCE. It is often believed that the Edomites, who towards the end of the monarchic period had begun to expand westwards into the eastern Negev (Beit-Arieh

1989; Stern 2001: 268–94), assisted the Babylonians during their campaign against Judah (Lemaire 2010: 236–40). They might even have been responsible for the destruction of Arad, Kadesh-Barnea and other Judean towns in the Negev (Mazar 1990: 460).

One of the main reasons for connecting Obadiah to the exilic period is the explosion of anti-Edomite sentiment in OT texts from the sixth century onwards. Lamentations, which deals with the trauma of the destruction of Jerusalem, singles out Edom for a special criticism (Lam. 4.21-22). It is likely that the 'sword in the wilderness' (Lam. 5.9), which endangers the survival of the Judean community, is also a veiled reference to the Edomites. Psalm 137.7-9 places Edom in parallel with Babylon and speaks of both peoples with equal bitterness and hatred. Indictments against Edom are found in prophetic OAN from the exilic period (Amos 1.11-12; Ezek. 25), but there are also increasingly passages that focus exclusively on Edom (Amos 9.12; Ezek. 35; 36.4-5; Isa. 34; 63.1-7; cf. Joel 3.19-20). Edomite involvement in Judah's troubles during the sixth century is the most plausible explanation for such a widespread bitterness against Edom from that period on.

Bartlett has challenged this hypothesis, pointing out that there is no hard evidence to support it. The charges against Edom are not specific enough to be tied to the events of 587 BCE. Jeremiah and Kings do not allude to any Edomite collusion with the Babylonians; in fact Jer. 40.11 suggests precisely the opposite. The destruction of Arad, like that of other major cities in Judah, could have been caused by the Babylonians (Bartlett 1989: 150–7; Ben Zvi 1996a: 236 n. 22). Tebes (2011) argues that the Edomite crimes are an example of a 'stab-in-the-back' myth which arose out of the feelings of national humiliation following a major military defeat and the need to find a minority group which functions as a scapegoat.

Na'aman (2016) has recently examined in some detail Bartlett's argument and found it unconvincing. According to him, the archaeological evidence suggests that the relationship between Judah and Edom throughout the seventh century was marked by peaceful cooperation under the auspices of the Assyrian Empire. This changed in the sixth century when Edom began to pose an increasing threat. An early indication of this can be found in Jer. 13.19, which reflects fears of a possible Edomite attack on the Negev. The decisive evidence comes from the Arad ostraca. These are letters written on potsherds that were discovered during the archaeological excavations of the southern Judean fortress city of Arad. Many of them date from around the beginning of the sixth century and deal with administrative and military matters. Ostracon 24 contains an order to a certain Eliashib to dispatch a contingent of soldiers as reinforcement to Ramath-negeb 'lest anything happen to the city ... lest (the) Edom(ites) (should) enter there' (*COS* 3.43K). The letters, more broadly, indicate that the western mercenaries serving in the Judean army (the *kittim*) were stationed in the Negev to defend the southern border of the kingdom, and, according to Na'aman, testify to the severity of the crisis occasioned by Edomite military pressure. Therefore, the traditional theory of an Edomite attack on Judah in conjunction with the Babylonian conquest still provides the best explanation of the historical background of Obadiah (Barton 2001: 120–3, 149; Renkema 2003: 33–6).

The punishment of Edom (vv. 7-9)

Archaeological excavations indicate that a number of sites in Edom suffered destruction during the sixth century BCE (Bartlett 1989: 158–9; Stern 2001: 325–6, 330–1). During the third year of his reign, the Babylonian king Nabonidus (556–539 BCE) led a campaign against Tema in Arabia (*ANET* 313). A fragmentary note in the Nabonidus Chronicle (*ANET* 305), which speaks of the siege of a town in *[]dummu* in the third year, may suggest that en route to Tema Nabonidus attacked Edom (Lindsay 1976: 32–9; Crowell 2007: 78–80). A rock relief of Nabonidus, dated to his fifth year (551 BCE), near Edomite es-Sela' confirms such a campaign against Edom (Crowell 2007: 80–3). Na'aman (2016: 30) conjectures that Nabonidus campaigned twice, in 553 and 551 BCE. It is likely that these campaigns brought the end of the kingdom of Edom (Raabe 1996: 54; Crowell 2007: 84–5; Lemaire 2010: 240–3). If correct, this reconstruction would tie in well with the threats of Obadiah. Verse 8 states that Edom's allies will deceive and overpower him. This could be a reference to the Babylonians with whom Edom had allied itself earlier.

The date(s) of Obadiah

On the basis of the above, it is best, with most commentators, to date Obad. 1-14, 15b to the sixth century, and to see it as a response to the Edomite participation in the Babylonian destruction of Judah (Wolff 1986: 18; Mason 1991: 94; Raabe 1996: 51–5; Barton 2001: 123; Jenson 2008: 4–5). Some attempt greater precision and date the book to the middle of the sixth

century on the grounds that it was composed in relation to the campaigns of
Nabonidus (Renkema 2003: 32–3; Na'aman 2016: 30–1).

One piece of information does not fit this dating very well. Verse 20
mentions Sepharad as one of the places where the exiled Jews live. Sepharad
is to be identified with Sardes, the capital of Lydia in western Asia Minor (for
a discussion see Raabe 1996: 268–70 and Pons 2014). A memorial stele
testifies to the presence of Jewish settlers in western Asia Minor from the
mid-fifth century BCE (Wolff 1986: 67–8), but there is no indication that a
Jewish colony existed there as early as the first half of the sixth century. There
are several ways in which this difficulty can be resolved. Those who date
Obadiah in the sixth century and regard the book as a unity (i) place
Sepharad in Mesopotamia (Stuart 1987: 421; Block 2017: 104), (ii) assume
that Jewish exiles were settled in Asia Minor already in the sixth century
(Allen 1976: 13; Jenson 2008: 26) or (iii) regard v. 20 as later interpolation
(Renkema 2003: 214–15). Alternatively some scholars argue for a fifth-
century date for the entire composition (Nogalski 2011: 367–8). The
description of Edom's demise in vv. 5-7 is taken not as a prediction but as a
past event, connected somehow to the devastation referred to in Mal. 1.1-4
and alludes to the Arab pressure on the Edomite territory from the fifth
century BCE onwards (Bewer 1911: 7–8; Jeremias 2007: 57–8).

As shown above, there are reasons to believe that vv. 15a, 16-21 constitute
a series of additions to the original prophetic book. The sixth century serves
as the historical background only of the first half of Obadiah. The finished
text represents a more complex composition which, in its totality, is
somewhat removed from the traumatic events that initially gave rise to the
prophecy.

Further study

On the history of Edom see Bartlett 1989 and Lemaire 2010. The economy
and society of Edom are discussed by Tebes 2014. On Edom's interaction
with Judah and Babylon see Lindsay 1976; Stern 2001; Crowell 2007;
Na'aman 2016. On the date of Obadiah see the surveys and discussions in
Raabe 1996; Renkema 2003; Barton 2001; Jenson 2008. On Sepharad see
Wolff 1986: 67–8; Raabe 1996: 268–70; Pons 2014. Niehaus 1993 is one of the
few contemporary scholars to argue for a pre-exilic date. For a fifth-century
date see Nogalski 2011.

8

The genre, setting and purpose of Obadiah

Chapter Outline

Further study   51

Insofar as the main theme of Obadiah revolves around the condemnation of Edom, the book resembles the oracles against the nations (OAN) found in Isaiah 13–23, Jeremiah 46–51, Ezekiel 25–32, Amos 1–2 and Zephaniah 2. Its closest parallel is Nahum which likewise has a single focus: the judgement of Nineveh. In fact, those interpreters who maintain that the book of the Twelve is conceived as a single composition think that within it Obadiah and Nahum play a role analogous to the role of the OAN sections in the Major Prophets.

Two backgrounds have been proposed for the emergence of the OAN: war and worship. Christensen (1975) traces the development of the OAN from the war oracles in ancient Israel (see also Albertz 2003a: 182–3). More recently, Hagedorn (2007) has compared Greek and Israelite prophecies against foreigners on the assumption that their context is that of war. On the other hand, Geyer (2004, 2009) argues for a consistently cultic origin of the main OAN tradition. As part of the liturgy for the New Year festival, the OAN are to be understood against the mythological background of Yahweh's battle with chaos which led to the proclamation of Yahweh's kingship and the purification of the temple.

The profound changes in Judean life introduced by the exile mean that neither of these proposals is directly applicable to the book of Obadiah. Whatever their role in the monarchic period, after the destruction of Jerusalem the OAN must have functioned in a different way than before.

With regard to Ezekiel's OAN, Lee (2016) argues that the foreign nations there parallel Judah and contribute to a universal picture of Yahweh's judgement on human wickedness. Crouch (2011) suggests that the motif of Yahweh's victory over the forces of chaos, personified by Egypt and Tyre, was used to address the questions about Yahweh's status and power occasioned by the defeat of Judah. Such overt mythological themes are not explicit in Obadiah, but the final form of the book links the triumph of Jacob over Esau with the kingship of Yahweh (v. 21).

Albertz (2003a: 183–8) thinks that pre-exilic OAN explored Yahweh's universal power and sovereignty in history but after 587 BCE the devastation of Judah's enemies began more consistently to serve to express a message of salvation. A number of commentators see such an implicit message as the main point of Obadiah's prophecy (Stuart 1987: 408; Block 2017: 35). This is based on the assumption that while the apparent audience are the Edomites, the real audience of the prophecy throughout are the Judean community (Jenson 2008: 10-1). Raabe (1995, 1996: 56-60) is an exception to this approach. He proposes that Obadiah also addresses the Edomites and tries to persuade them to desist from future hostile actions.

In terms of Obadiah's social location two different solutions are offered by scholars: the cult and scribal activity. The view of Watts (1969: 20-7; 1975: 5-8, 51) that Obadiah was a liturgical text that formed a part of the ritual of the New Year festival in the Second Temple has not gained wide acceptance, but the more general position that Obadiah was a cultic prophet is popular (Coggins 1985: 69; Barton 2001: 124). According to Wolff (1986: 19-21) he ministered in the context of the lamentation services held at the site of the ruined temple in Jerusalem. During such services the laments of the congregation were answered by cultic prophets like Obadiah, who assured the people that Yahweh had heard their prayers (see also Albertz 2003a: 188–94; Ogden 1982).

Renkema (2003: 26-9) argues strongly against the hypothesis of Obadiah's cultic connections. He assumes that all cultic prophets would have been discredited by the events of 587 BCE and prefers to see Obadiah as a 'preacher at work in the community's inner circle who expanded and actualized the older prophetic tradition' (2003: 27). According to Jeremias (2007: 57-60) Obadiah is a scribal prophet whose book must be regarded as an 'exegesis' of Jer. 49.7-16. The composition of the book was inspired by the conviction that current events constituted a partial fulfilment of earlier prophecies (Jer. 49.7-16) and served as a sign that the universal judgement of the end is approaching (see already Bewer 1911: 13–14).

These proposals correspond in some degree to the different stages of the evolution of the book. It is reasonable to conceive Obadiah's activity that led to the writing of vv. 1-14, 15b in connection with the cult in Judah during the sixth century. The additions that sought to universalize and reinterpret the prophecy beyond the confines of its immediate historical horizon bear the marks of scribal exegesis.

Further study

On the OAN in Israel see Christensen 1975; Raabe 1995; Albertz 2003a; Geyer 2004, 2009; Hagedorn 2007; Crouch 2011; Lee 2016. On Obadiah as a cultic prophet consult Watts 1969, 1975; Ogden 1982; Wolff 1986; Albertz 2003a and contrast Renkema 2003. On Obadiah as a scribal prophecy see Jeremias 2007 and in addition Nogalski 1993b; Dicou 1994.

9

Edom and the image of the other

Chapter Outline

Ways of understanding and interpreting Obadiah's invective	52
Hermeneutical strategies for reading Obadiah	54
Further study	55

'Obadiah is hard to love,' says John Barton. 'It seems to contain very little beyond a xenophobic hatred of other nations and of Edom in particular' (Barton 2001: 126). This quote exemplifies well the problem many contemporary readers have with the book. How do we make sense of, and find value in, a text whose main topic is the condemnation of a treacherous 'brother' and the anticipation of his deserved destruction?

Ways of understanding and interpreting Obadiah's invective

Looking at Obadiah from a purely historical point of view it is not difficult to understand its vitriolic attack on Edom against the background of the events of 587 BCE and their aftermath. According to Dicou (1994: 182–97) Edom's actions at the time of the Babylonian conquest and its subsequent occupation of Judean territories were remembered in the lamentation services (on the evidence for such services see Albertz 2003a: 141) of the exilic period and gave rise to the bitterness against it. Working on a more theological level, Anderson (2011: 186–94) argues for a focus on two themes: brotherhood and land. First, Edom betrayed his brother; that is, he failed to live up to the obligations that his special relationship with Judah entailed. Second, the Edomites occupied the land that Yahweh had given to his people as an inheritance and thus committed an offence not just against fellow human beings but against Yahweh himself.

OAN play an important role in identity politics. They draw lines between 'us' and 'them' and can be especially significant when historical events threaten a group's identity (Hagedorn 2011a: 434–7; Claassens 2016: 338–40). Assis (2006, 2016) understands the anti-Edomite polemic of Obadiah within this framework. The events of 587 BCE, interpreted as divine abandonment, struck at the very core of Israel's sense of self-identity and questioned its position as a divinely chosen nation. The threat posed by Edom stemmed precisely from his status as Israel's rival brother which meant it could undermine Israel's special place as a chosen nation after its divine rejection.

Even though such considerations may help us understand Obadiah's polemic they do not solve the problem entirely. As Coggins (1985: 76, 101–2) points out, the book portrays evil and arrogance as a force embodied in real-life human beings, the Edomites and so breeds intolerance and hatred towards people who are different. O'Brien (2008: 161–73) offers an ideological critique of the motif of brotherhood, which is commonly seen as providing a legitimate basis for Obadiah's grievances. She argues that the language of brotherhood could be used as a tool of coercion against one's opponents. The metaphor manipulatively suggests that Judah's interests need to be shared and upheld by Edom and denies any responsibility on Judah's part for establishing, maintaining and developing the brotherly relationship with its neighbour.

Traditionally the usefulness of Obadiah was achieved primarily by means of allegorical readings. In Jewish tradition Edom was identified with the Roman Empire, responsible for the destruction of the Second Temple, and subsequently with Christianity which claimed to have taken Israel's place as the new people of God (Assis 2016: 175–87). A similar tendency is exhibited by early Christian writers who take Edom as a reference to the devil, the heretics or the works of the flesh (Ferreiro 2003: 119–27). In modern times the drive to solve the moral issues by de-historicizing Edom continues to be strong. The Edomites cease to be a specific group of people and instead become a representation of actions and attitudes that are generally regarded as reprehensible, like pride, betrayal and greed (Jenson 2008: 8; see also Mason 1991: 107).

Hermeneutical strategies for reading Obadiah

The way the message of the book is construed and appropriated depends primarily on the prior ethical and theological commitments of the reader. These commitments will dictate how a reader will identify with the main characters of the prophecy – Judah and Edom. If a community imagines that it stands in symbolic continuity with the Judean audience of the book, its enemies can easily be regarded as the wicked 'Edomites' who are to be punished and destroyed. The book then can be used to justify hatred of the other on the grounds of real or imagined grievances. It may even sanction physical violence, because, after all, the fire that devours and destroys Esau comes from the 'house of Joseph' (v. 18). However, we need to bear in mind that the implied audience of Obadiah are victims of violence and abuse. For them the trauma is a present reality and the reversal of fortunes still lies in the future. On that basis Adu-Gyamfi (2015) argues that the message of Obadiah is that God is on the side of the victims of ethnic hatred. People who are in a position of power cannot legitimately appropriate the book, only those who experience betrayal and defeat. A responsible reading of Obadiah does not allow anyone indiscriminately to identify themselves with the Judean readership.

A different strategy is available to those readers who are not in a state of humiliation, powerlessness and pain. They can identify not with Judah but with the antagonist, Edom. Two examples, an ancient and a modern one, illustrate how such a strategy might work. In his prayer for his ministry as a bishop, Ambrose asks God for the ability to

> mourn with those who sin; for this is a great virtue, since it is written: 'And you shall not rejoice over the children of Judah in the day of their destruction and speak not proudly in the day of trouble.' Grant that so often as the sin of anyone who has fallen is made known to me I may suffer with him and not chide him proudly but mourn and weep. (Ferreiro 2003: 122)

Here Ambrose in effect identifies himself with Edom, addressed by the imperatives of Obadiah 12–14. He takes the attitudes and actions of Edom not as an indictment of what he has done in the past but as a warning of what he might be tempted to do in the future: rejoice over the troubles of others, or even misuse those troubles for his own gain. As he moves into a position of power, the Edomite transgression becomes an ever-present danger in his own life, an example how not to behave, and a challenge to a lifestyle of compassion.

Snyman (2016) offers a reading from the context of post-apartheid South Africa. In such a context the perpetrators of crimes can read Obadiah from the vantage point of the Edomites. In the prophecy Edom is silent, but it is proper that he is not given a voice, because Obadiah provides Edom, the perpetrator, with an opportunity to listen and so to see his own crimes from the perspective of his victim. The book is a challenge to hear and accept the brother's critique and to confront one's own past misdeeds against a vulnerable other.

Therefore, how one chooses to read Obadiah, whether as Edom or Judah, depends on a combination of the reader's situation and their chosen hermeneutical framework. Obadiah informs our attitude towards the other not in a vacuum but in the context of our overall experience of life and our ethical commitments.

Further study

For historical explanations of Obadiah's anti-Edomite polemic see Dicou 1994 and Assis 2016. A theological treatment of the issue can be found in Renkema 2003; Jenson 2008; Anderson 2011. O'Brien 2008 provides ideological criticism of the book. For Obadiah's reception history consult Ferreiro 2003; Anderson 2013–2014; Assis 2016. A different reading through the lenses of a 'hermeneutic of vulnerability' is offered by Snyman 2016. Consult also Adu-Gyamfi 2015.

Part Three

Habakkuk

10 Interpretation problems in the book of Habakkuk

11 The righteous and the wicked: The contexts and meaning of Habakkuk 1–2

12 The prayer of Habakkuk (chapter 3)

13 Theodicy, empire and violence: Reflections on the theology of Habakkuk

Interpretation problems in the book of Habakkuk

Chapter outline

The oracle in 1.1	60
The connection of 1.2-4, 1.5-11 and 1.12-17	60
The vision in 2.1-4(5)	61
The identity of the wicked in the woe oracles 2.(5)6-20	62
The prayer (3.1-19)	63
Further study	64

The book of Habakkuk is a dialogue between a prophet and his God that addresses the issues of violence, justice and divine intervention in human affairs. It begins with a prophetic cry to Yahweh (1.2-4), continues with a divine answer in the form of a vision (2.1-4) and culminates in a prayer, which depicts a powerful theophany (3.1-19).

A more detailed understanding of the text requires ability to identify its constituent parts and decide how they relate to each other. Unfortunately, this is not easy at all as far as Habakkuk is concerned. At the macro level the book, with its two superscriptions, falls naturally into two main parts: an oracle in chapters one and two and a prayer in chapter three (Sweeney 1991a: 63–5, 2000a: 457–8). Most scholars prefer to have three major sections, although there is disagreement on the place of 2.1-4. Some take it with chapter one and have a dialogue in 1.2–2.4 followed by a series of woe oracles in 2.5-20 (Rudolph 1975: 195; Perlitt 2004: 42; Dietrich 2016). Others link it to chapter two and argue for a complaint in 1.2-17 followed by a report of an oracular inquiry in 2.1-20 (Floyd 2000: 81–2; Prinsloo 1999).

When we move to the micro level the task becomes much more difficult. Even though there the boundaries of the various subunits are clear enough, their interconnection is often fraught with ambiguity. To complicate things even further, the meaning of some key terms and grammatical constructions in the text of Habakkuk is uncertain. Below is a sample of the most vexing difficulties.

The oracle in 1.1

The precise meaning of the very first word, which designates the book as an 'oracle' (*maśśā'*), is disputed. Some regard it as a term for a prophecy of destruction usually directed against a foreign nation (Schneider 1979: 177–8; Smith 1984: 98; Perlitt 2004: 5; Dietrich 2016: 106), others as an oracle, which seeks to explain an earlier revelation (Weis 1992; Sweeney 1991a: 65; Floyd 2000: 85–6, 2002). From the start, we are not sure what exactly it is we are reading.

The connection of 1.2-4, 1.5-11 and 1.12-17

There is little doubt that chapter one consists of three different subsections. The prophet speaks in 1.2-4, God speaks in 1.5-11 and the prophet speaks again in 1.12-17. The transition from Habakkuk's complaint in 1.2-4 to the divine oracle in 1.5-11 is very abrupt. There is no explicit indication how the content of the oracle relates to the preceding complaint. Most scholars assume that this is God's answer to Habakkuk and on that basis construe 1.2–2.4 as a dialogue between God and the prophet (Thompson 1993; Moseman 2017; Thomas 2018: 62). Mack (2011) draws attention to a Neo-Assyrian text containing a dialogue between King Ashurbanipal and the god Nabu which may provide a parallel. However, 1.5-11 does not read like an answer to 1.2-4. It is directed to the nation as a whole, not to the prophet who speaks in vv. 2-4. Moreover, it does not address the issues of injustice and 'promises' to solve the problem of violence by announcing the arrival of more violence.

One possible solution is that here Habakkuk is quoting (Floyd 1991; 2000: 95–9; Prinsloo 2004: 631–2), or providing a 'flashback' (Cleaver-Bartholomew 2004: 48–9), to an earlier oracle (Wellhausen 1898: 166). However, there are no indications in the text that a quote follows in 1.5.

Another option is that vv. 5-11 are not a real reply from Yahweh but a parody of Jer. 5.15-17 (Markl 2004:105–6). However, does that mean it is impossible to understand Habakkuk on its own terms without knowledge of Jeremiah? Alternatively, the verses could be a continuation and intensification of the complaint. They show the international aspect, or cause, of the violence lamented in the previous passage (Dangl 2014: 47–8), or yet another problem that troubles the prophet (Cathcart 2010: 340). Yet, the change of speaker in 1.5-6 does not make this a natural reading of the text. On the level of content and flow of thought the relationship between the two passages remains ambiguous, and it is possible that no organic relationship exists between these two fragments (Perlitt 2004: 47–8).

Relating 1.12-17 to its larger context is equally problematic. Are these verses the prophet's response to the divine speech in 1.5-11, as many scholars assume, or a continuation of the complaint from 1.2-4 (Cleaver-Bartholomew 2004: 56 n. 35), or a parallel complaint to the one in 1.2-4 (Eaton 1981: 60; Haak 1992: 15)? The decision whether to construe 1.2–2.4 as a dialogue between Yahweh and the prophet or to take 1.2-17 as a unified complaint by the prophet addressed to Yahweh is fundamental for understanding what is going on in this passage. The problem is that the text provides no clear guidance to help with this decision.

The vision in 2.1-4(5)

In this passage Habakkuk is promised a vision and instructed to write down this vision and await its fulfilment. The text, however, does not make explicit what the vision is. Different parts of the book have been proposed as the contents of the vision: the oracle about the coming of the Chaldeans in 1.5-11 (Dietrich 2016: 127–8; cf. Seybold 1991: 57); the woe oracles proclaiming the future judgement on Babylon in 2.6-20 (Andersen 2001: 221–2); the vision in 3.3-15 (Roberts, 1991: 149; Gafney 2017: 107). While these suggestions differ on the precise identification of the material which constituted the vision, they all agree on the main point: the message of the vision had to do with the ultimate downfall of the Babylonians.

Another possibility is that the received vision, or oracle, is to be found in 2.4(-5) (Sweeney 2000a: 471–2; Floyd 2000: 113–14). The translation and interpretation of these verses is notoriously difficult (Pinker 2007; Renz 2013). Part of the problem is the ambiguity of the last two words of 2.4

(Hunn 2009). The Hebrew verb 'he will live' could be understood as 'he will survive' or 'he will pursue a certain type of lifestyle', and the word *'emûnātô* can depict the quality of the righteous person ('his faith/faithfulness') or of the vision ('its trustworthiness'). Many scholars believe that 2.4 refers to the contrasting fates of two different groups of people (Haak 1992: 59; Dietrich 2016: 129–30). For example, Emerton (1977: 10–17) translates, 'Behold, he whose personality within him is not upright will fly away (i.e. perish), but the righteous man will live because of his faithfulness,' while Cathcart (2010: 350), following Rudolph, suggests: 'Behold, there is punishment for the man whose soul is not upright in him, but the righteous man will live because of his faithfulness.' If this is correct, then 2.4 could potentially be regarded as the revelation received by Habakkuk in his vision. Others, however, argue that 2.4 describes two possible responses to the vision. Roberts (1991: 105–12) translates, 'Now the fainthearted, his soul will not walk in it [i.e. the vision],/ But the righteous person will live by its [i.e. the vision's] faithfulness.' In other words, those who do not follow the admonition of 2.3 to 'wait' for the fulfilment of the vision do not pursue a 'manner of life consistent with the message of the vision', while the righteous accept the vision's truthfulness and trust in the promises of God.

The identity of the wicked in the woe oracles 2.(5)6-20

The woe oracles in chapter two present different pictures of this wicked person. He gives out loans and charges interest (2.7), receives unjust gain (2.9), builds a city with blood (2.12), makes his neighbour drunk in order to gaze at his nakedness (2.15), commits violence (2.8, 17) and worships idols (2.19). These wicked deeds lead to an inevitable downfall. His creditors will rise against him and the nations will plunder him (2.7-8), the cup of Yahweh's wrath will encircle him and his shame will be exposed (2.16). The oracles are very general and do not clarify who this wicked person is. The reference to plundering nations suggests that the wicked might be either the Babylonian king or a collective representation of the Babylonian nation. The links to the description of the Chaldeans in chapter one ('what is not his' = *lō' lô*; 1.6, 2.6) confirms this.

However, some of the details of the woe oracles do not fit neatly with this interpretation, because they are not suitable for describing the atrocities of an imperial power. Acquiring other people's possessions by means of unfair lending practices (2.6b) and making 'unjust gain' (2.9) are social evils committed by rich people against members of their own community, not by a world empire against conquered populations. The actions of the person who 'builds a city with blood and establishes a town with wickedness' (2.12) conspicuously remind one of Jeremiah's indictments against King Jehoiakim who built 'his house with unrighteousness … [making] his neighbours work for nothing' (Jer. 22.13).

The prayer (3.1-19)

The final section opens with its own superscription which mirrors 1.1 and designates what follows as 'a prayer of Habakkuk the prophet'. It leaves the reader uncertain how to relate the two major sections of the book: the oracle (1.1–2.20) and the prayer (3.1-19). Are they to be read as two independent works because of the two separate superscriptions, or should we strive to find some connection between them because both mention Habakkuk?

Chapter three contains many sections where the Hebrew is almost unintelligible, because either the text is damaged or our knowledge of the language is imperfect. The prayer is said to be 'according to *šigyōnōṯ*' (cf. Ps. 7.1), a term which may denote 'lament song' (Sweeney 2000a: 458, 480) or a 'wild, passionate song, with rapid changes of rhythm' (*BDB* 993; cf. 'staggering rhythm' Mathews 2012: 144, 150), that is, the song of an ecstatic (cf. *HALOT* 4:1414). It is also possible that the meaning of this term is no longer accessible to us (see the detailed discussion in Andersen 2001: 268–73).

The appearance of Yahweh at the start (3.3-4) may be intended to evoke the image of a sunrise (Lortie 2016: 97–102) or the arrival of a storm (Roberts 1991: 152–4). He could be either a sun-god (if *'ôr* in 3.4 is understood to refer to 'sun-light'), with rays (*qarnayim*) coming from his side, hiding his power in the midst of his unbearable brightness (Rudolph 1975: 234, 243), or a storm-god (if *'ôr* in 3.4 is understood to refer to 'lightning') holding a double-pronged bolt (*qarnayim*) in his hand, who pierces briefly the darkness with a flash and then hides again his power in the thick stormy clouds that cover the sky (Roberts).

The bulk of the theophany contains Yahweh's battle with an enemy, but many of the details are uncertain. Verse 9 is almost impossible to translate. Does it say that Yahweh is shooting arrows that are sated with blood as they find their targets (Roberts 1991: 139–40, 155)? Or is Yahweh bringing here into view another weapon alongside the bow – his seven maces (Andersen 2001: 320–5)? Or does it depict Yahweh preparing for battle by speaking oaths on, or empowering by enchantment, his battle rods (Haak 1992: 94–5; Lortie 2016: 112–13)? Likewise it is not entirely clear what exactly it is that Yahweh smashes in v. 13b. It could be the house of the wicked (either literally, that is, the palace, or metaphorically, that is, the royal dynasty; Koenen 1994: 143–4) whose foundations are laid bare; or it could be the body of the chaos monster who is slain (Hiebert 1986: 103–4).

A new and surprising development comes with 3.17: a description of an all-encompassing crop failure and the death of all cattle. It is again not clear how this agricultural disaster is related to the preceding military confrontation. Is this a traditional ANE trope that conveys the idea of the absence of the deity (Haak 1992: 17–8; Cathcart 2010: 345)? Is it nature's response to the theophany described in the previous verses (Hiebert 1986: 114)? Is it a description of the devastating effects of the Babylonian invasion on the land of Judah (O'Neal 2007: 119; Lortie 2016: 134–6)? Is it a way of portraying the 'worst-case scenario', even more bitter than the Babylonian oppression (Roberts 1991: 157), or a 'poetic foil for Habakkuk's confession of trust' (Gafney 2017: 114)? Or is it a description of the judgement which will fall upon 'those who attack us' from v. 16b (Koenen 1994:145; Barre 2013: 461)? The statement widens the application of the prayer to different types of crisis situation, adding economic hardship to the military threat of the previous verses.

Further study

The structure of the book is discussed by Sweeney 1991a; Prinsloo 1999; Dangl 2014. On the individual exegetical issues see the commentaries, especially Rudolph 1975; Roberts 1991; Sweeney 2000a; Andersen 2001; Nogalski 2011; Dietrich 2016; Gafney 2017. On *maśśāʾ* see Schneider 1979; Andersen 2001; Floyd 2002. For the genre of 'woe oracles' see the discussion of Floyd 2000 and the literature cited there. On chapter one as dialogue see Moseman 2017 and contrast Floyd 1991, 2000; Cleaver-Bartholomew 2004; Prinsloo 2004. On the text and translation of 2.4 see Emerton 1977; Pinker 2007; Hunn 2009; Renz 2013. On chapter three consult Hiebert 1986 and Lortie 2016.

11

The righteous and the wicked: The contexts and meaning of Habakkuk 1–2

Chapter Outline

The historical context(s) of Habakkuk	65
The wicked are Judeans	68
The wicked are a foreign nation	69
Redactional changes in the identity of the wicked	70
Habakkuk and cultic prophecy	71
Further study	72

The historical context(s) of Habakkuk

A key interpretative issue which has a major bearing on how one understands the overall thrust of the text of Habakkuk is determining the identity of the wicked and the righteous in chs 1–2. The decision on this matter is influenced by how one reconstructs the historical context of the prophecy.

The only piece of historical information Habakkuk offers is the mention of the Chaldeans in 1.6. Virtually everybody sees 1.6 as a reference to the rise of Babylon under the leadership of Nabopolassar and his son Nebuchadnezzar. Consequently, many date the ministry of the prophet and the writing of his oracles to the end of the seventh or the beginning of the sixth century BCE, just after the collapse of the Assyrian Empire. Judah's inability to adjust to this new international situation ultimately resulted in the capture of

Jerusalem by the Babylonians, the destruction of the temple and the end of the Davidic monarchy. Most scholars place the oracles of Habakkuk a few years prior to that, during the reign of Jehoiakim, and see this as the primary context within which they are to be interpreted: 608–5 BCE (Robertson 1990: 34–7; cf. Barker/Bailey 1998: 260); 605–597 BCE (Rudolph 1975: 194); 608–597 BCE (Szeles 1987: 5; Chitsulo 2015: 311–2); 605–603 BCE (Haak 1992); shortly after 605 BCE (Sweeney 2000a: 455). Some would allow for a longer timespan: from 609 BCE to some time after 597 BCE (Roberts 1991: 82–4); 605–575 BCE (Andersen 2001: 27).

Judean kings	Major events
Josiah (640–609 BCE)	Fall of Nineveh (612 BCE) – end of the Assyrian Empire
Jehoahaz (609 BCE)	Death of King Josiah at the hands of the Egyptian king Necho (609 BCE) – Jehoahaz deposed by Necho and taken to Egypt
Jehoiakim (609–597 BCE)	Battle of Carchemish, Babylon defeats Egypt (605 BCE) – Judah becomes vassal to Babylon
Jehoiachin (597 BCE)	First siege of Jerusalem by the Babylonians (597 BCE) – Jehoiachin deposed by Nebuchadnezzar and taken to Babylon
Zedekiah (597–587 BCE)	Second siege of Jerusalem (587/586 BCE) – the temple destroyed and Judah incorporated into the Babylonian Empire

Many who agree with such a dating of Habakkuk's ministry believe that the book itself is an exilic or post-exilic creation and needs to be read against that later historical background. Among such scholars there are two main models of the redactional development of Habakkuk. According to the first, the vision announcing the end of the Assyrian Empire (1.5-11, 14-17, 2.1-3) and a shorter version of the woe oracles criticizing certain social and economic trends in Judah (2.5-19*) come from the preaching of the pre-exilic prophet. Together with the hymn of chapter three, these were reworked during the sixth century (550 BCE [Seybold] or 520 BCE [Albertz]) and used as a basis for the first edition of the book. This exilic composition sought to interpret history by pronouncing judgement on the Babylonian empire for its atrocities and giving hope to the people of Judah. The lament passages (1.2-4, 12-13; 2.4, 20; 3.13b-14, 17-19a) formed an independent lament Psalm from the post-exilic period which was incorporated at some later stage (Seybold 1991: 43–9; Albertz 2003a: 237–45).

The second redactional model reverses the supposed early and late materials: it treats the laments as belonging to the early layer and the anti-Babylonian passages as later insertions. According to one version of this proposal, the ground-text coming from the prophet consisted of three sections: the lament about violence and oppression (1.2-4, 13), the reception of a vision responding to this lament (2.1-4) and five brief woe oracles against the wicked which answer the lament (2.6b, 9, 12, 15, 19). This text was reworked twice, during the sixth and the fifth centuries BCE, adding the passages about the rise of the Babylonians (1.5-12, 14-17) and giving an international dimension to the woe oracles (Lescow 1995: 73–82; cf. Koenen 1994: 124–40; differently Dietrich 2016: 98–101). In spite of the differences with the first model, the overall picture that emerges is remarkably similar. The social criticism of Habakkuk, directed at the Judean upper class in the pre-exilic period, was transformed into a criticism of the Babylonian empire in the exilic period.

The mention of the Chaldeans in 1.6 is sometimes regarded as a later gloss (Seybold 1991: 58). Therefore, initially the invaders were anonymous and the oracle (1.5-11) loses its historical rootedness. Pfeiffer (2005: 135–51) and Hagedorn (2015) think that originally it depicted the Persians and provided a theological explanation for the rise of the Persian Empire. This pushes the dating of Habakkuk into the Persian period. Nogalski (1993b: 136–46, 150-4) thinks the original composition of Habakkuk was a 'wisdom oriented layer' coming from the early post-exilic period, which was supplemented by a 'Babylonian commentary' sometime later as the script was being tied to the book of the Twelve. Similar reconstruction is offered by Wöhrle (2008a: 291–322) for whom the original layer focused on the conflict between the godly and the sinners and reflected the social crisis within the Judean community during the fifth century BCE.

Mack (2011) severs completely the link between Habakkuk and the monarchic period. He argues that there is a stark difference between the text of Habakkuk and the Neo-Assyrian prophecies from the seventh century BCE. Habakkuk betrays no interest in the Judean politics of the pre-exilic period and no signs of monarchical patronage. The king and his enemies are not the focus of attention of the prophecy. The book is not propagandistic in nature, but is a literary work, which transforms earlier genres and employs a variety of sophisticated literary devices. There was no complicated redactional process leading up to its composition and no orally proclaimed message standing behind it. Instead, Habakkuk is to be taken as a scribal literary composition, which utilized traditional, free-floating phrases and motifs. It sought to respond to the destruction of Jerusalem and provide an authoritative, divine interpretation of history (Mack, 2011: 272–80, 326–39).

Herrmann (2001) wants to put the date of Habakkuk even later, to the Greek period. In his view the language is late and the book betrays familiarity with a wide variety of OT traditions. The description of the fast and unstoppable conquerors (1.5-11), going east (1.9), is inspired by the march of the Greeks under Alexander the Great, not by the Babylonians, whose mention in 1.6 is to be regarded as cypher rather than as a pointer to the original historical situation of the text. Habakkuk is close to apocalyptic literature, which anticipates the worldwide destruction of the sinners and calls the faithful to wait patiently for the end.

Scholars, therefore, disagree about the historical context of the book of Habakkuk. Some think exclusively in terms of the monarchic period. Others envisage a redactional process, which begins before the exile, but stretches into the exilic and post-exilic periods. Still others look to the Persian or the Greek era as the time of composition. These different reconstructions impact the identification of the righteous and the wicked and the way the text of the prophecy is understood.

The wicked are Judeans

According to Haak (1992: 116–30; 138–49) the righteous and the wicked (1.4, 13) are not general categories, but references to specific individuals who, because of their association with law, order and justice, are best understood as royal figures. The righteous one is King Jehoahaz who took the throne for three months in 609 BCE after Josiah's death and who was deposed by the Egyptians. The wicked one is his brother Jehoiakim who became a king in his stead (1992: 112–13; 131–4). Habakkuk was a member of the anti-Egyptian, pro-Babylonian faction. He was supportive of Jehoahaz and expected his swift return to the throne. However, when this expectation was frustrated, Habakkuk wrote down the book to confirm that the original vision will be fulfilled and needs to be awaited.

One difficulty with Haak's proposal is that it requires the entire book to be interpreted as consistently pro-Babylonian, which is not the most natural way of reading the text. The suggestion that the wicked is the Judean king does not account sufficiently for the international scope of the wicked's activity (1.15-17 and 2.5-20). Most importantly, the idea that the righteous person has been displaced by a wicked contender and will return to the throne is nowhere to be found in the text of Habakkuk. It requires a lot of specific information to be read into language that is very general.

Most scholars believe that the identity of the wicked changes throughout the first chapter. In 1.2-4 problems internal to Judean society are in view and the wicked are members of the Judean royal court (Blenkinsopp 1996: 126; Roberts 1991: 89–90). In 1.5-11 God responds to the complaint about rampant injustice in Judah by announcing the coming of the Chaldeans who are going to bring judgement on his sinful people. Habakkuk reacts to this divine answer with horror and points out the cruelty of the Babylonians (1.12-17). From this point onwards the wicked in Habakkuk are the Chaldeans. The major problem with this interpretation is the difficulty, discussed in the previous chapter, of interpreting 1.5-11 as an answer to the complaint in 1.2-4.

The wicked are a foreign nation

Many argue that the wicked throughout the whole book, including 1.2-4, are a foreign power. One option, if one dates Habakkuk earlier in the seventh century (c. 640–630 BCE), is to identify the wicked as the Assyrians who oppress the righteous nation of Judah, still under their rule (Christensen 1975: 176, 179–80; Eaton 1981: 11, 59, 61). Others reach a similar conclusion not on the grounds of the presumed historical context, but because of Habakkuk's position within the book of the Twelve, after Nahum, which talks about Assyria (Schneider 1979: 52; Schart 1998: 245). Another option is to see the wicked as the Egyptians who controlled Jehoiakim and his court (Szeles 1987: 19; Haak 1992: 137–38; cf. Gafney 2017: 77).

More widespread is the position that the wicked in Habakkuk are the Babylonians. According to Johnson, 1.2-4 speak of foreign military oppression, which has led to the 'paralysis' of the Torah, understood as the deuteronomic text promulgated in the time of Josiah. The blessings that Deuteronomy promised as a reward for obedience had not become a reality, due to the violence of the Babylonian advance. In 1.5-11 nothing suggests that the Chaldeans are presented as the divine answer to the injustice Habakkuk sees. On the contrary, they are depicted negatively: they come for violence, their justice and dignity proceed from themselves, they worship their own strength. They are the cause of, rather than the answer to, the complaint (Johnson 1985: 260–4). Sweeney (2001: 308–10) suggests that

Habakkuk was critical of the Babylonian advance because he was supportive of Jehoiakim and viewed the Babylonian occupation of Judah after 605 BCE as a betrayal of the earlier alliance during the times of Hezekiah and Josiah.

According to Andersen (2001: 123, 180–9) the victims of the Babylonian oppression are neither the righteous remnant in Judah nor the nation of Judah as a whole. The righteous in both 1.2-4 and in 1.13 are the victims of the aggression of the wicked (i.e. the Babylonians), and as 1.17 makes clear these are all the nations. Thus the concern of the prophet is universal and his complaint is against the destructive violence of 'international imperialism'.

One problem with this position is that the conflict depicted in 1.2-4 does not seem on the face of it to have international dimensions. The terminology used in 1.2-4 is never applied in the Hebrew Bible to describe foreign powers (Dietrich 2016: 131–2), but often employed with reference to the ruling classes' exploitation of the poor. A number of details in the woe oracles (2.6-19) also do not fit very well the interpretation of the wicked person as the Babylonians because they seem to describe social injustice, not international imperialism.

Redactional changes in the identity of the wicked

The final form of the text invites the reader to see the wicked throughout as the Babylonians, but the way they are described in certain places (1.2-4 and parts of 2.6-17) suggests that they are Judean aristocrats. The most likely explanation for this phenomenon is that the material underwent a reworking, which altered the identity of the wicked and the righteous. During the late monarchy Habakkuk complained to Yahweh about the social abuses of the Judean upper class. He received a divine response and was instructed to write it down. The response was a series of woe oracles that proclaimed doom on those who exploit the poor. The first edition of the book, therefore, looked like this:

Habakkuk's complaint about violence and injustice	1.2-4, 12-14
Habakkuk waits for Yahweh's answer	2.1
Yahweh gives Habakkuk a vision and instructs him to write it down	2.2-4
The content of the vision: woe on the wicked	2.6b, 9, 12, 15, 19

After the destruction of Jerusalem this composition was reworked by the addition of the oracle in 1.5-11, 15-17 which depicts the violence of the Babylonian advance. It is possible that the insertions portrayed the Babylonians as Yahweh's tool for punishment of the sins of Judah, which in turn has incurred guilt by overstepping its mandate. However, it is equally possible that at this stage the exilic audience would have understood even the wicked in 1.2-4 as referring to the Babylonians. The same reworking can be observed in the woe oracles in chapter two. There a number of additions transform the literal description of social injustice into metaphors of illegitimate use of power in international affairs (Albertz 2003a: 239; Dietrich 2016: 151–6). For example, to the woe oracle that predicts the rise of the creditors against the person who accumulates wealth by means of unjust financial dealings (2.6b-7a) a saying is added (2.7b-8) that identifies those creditors with 'many nations' and the 'remaining peoples'. That addition reinterprets the giving of credits from 2.6b as a metaphor for bloodshed and violence in 2.8b.

Habakkuk and cultic prophecy

According to Sweeney, Habakkuk was a 'Temple-based oracle diviner … [who was] expected to present his oracles in a liturgical setting' (Sweeney 2000a: 456, 1991a: 70; cf. Lindblom 1967: 254; Eaton 1981: 11–14, 54–61; Blenkinsopp 1996: 126–8; Bruckner 2004: 202). This view is based on several considerations. The alternation between prayers of lament and oracles that answer them (1.2–2.4) reflects a liturgical sequence in which the prophet acts as a mediator between the people and God. The 'watchtower' in 2.1 could refer to a specially designated place in the temple where Habakkuk was waiting to receive his oracles. The title 'prophet' (1.1; 3.1) may imply a 'professional' or 'cultic' prophet. The description of Habakkuk's response to the received revelation in 3.16 points to involvement in ecstatic practices (Jeremias 1970: 90–107). However, not everyone agrees with this (Rudolph 1975: 194; Jöcken 1977: 515–17; Bellinger 1984: 83–6; Andersen 2001: 91–6). Bosshard-Nepustil (1997: 340–1) strikes a middle course. He thinks that the original layer (1.2-4, 12a, 13, 2.6b-16) was a cultic text, but the subsequent reworkings were not connected to the cult.

It is difficult, perhaps impossible, to come to a firm conclusion about the prophet's role in the temple worship. However, the general nature of his book suggests an effort to make it applicable beyond the narrow confines of the situation of pre-exilic Judah. The mention of the Babylonians in 1.6 anchors the origins of the prophecy in that particular historical context, but the book tends to speak in terms of the 'righteous' and the 'wicked' allowing later readers to relate its message to their own situation. This is not incompatible with what happens in the cult but it does not require that Habakkuk himself was a cultic functionary. It is possible to imagine that the exilic redaction of chs 1–2 was done with an eye on the needs of public worship and was somehow connected to the lamentation services that took place during that time.

Further study

On the different interpretations of the identity of the wicked in Habakkuk see Johnson 1985; Roberts 1991; Haak 1992; Floyd 2000; Andersen 2001. For survey of scholarship on the question see Jöcken 1977; Dangl 2001.

Helpful discussion of the redaction history of the book can be found in Nogalski 1993b; Koenen 1994; Albertz 2003a; Wöhrle 2008a; Dietrich 2016. For later dating of the book see especially Pfeiffer 2005; Mack 2011 and Herrmann 2001.

On Habakkuk's relation to the cult see Jeremias 1970; Eaton 1981; contrast Jöcken 1977; Bellinger 1984; Andersen 2001.

12

The prayer of Habakkuk (chapter 3)

Chapter Outline

The connection of chapter three to chapters one and two	73
Date and provenance of chapter three	76
Conclusion	78
Further study	78

The final chapter of Habakkuk presents a number of problems of its own. Its genre is unclear. Scholars have taken it to be a victory song (Hiebert 1986: 118–19), a lament (Haak 1992: 16–19), an individual prayer of thanksgiving (Roberts 1991: 149–50), a liturgy for the autumn festival (Smith 1984: 115), a hymn converted into a lament (Anderson 2011: 64), a prayer for Yahweh's intervention (Lortie 2016: 76–81). More importantly, its connection to the preceding material and its overall place and function in the book are a matter of debate.

The connection of chapter three to chapters one and two

Some believe that chapter three forms an integral part of Habakkuk, because it reflects the same concerns as chapters one and two and forms an indispensable conclusion to the book. The psalm talks about Yahweh's 'work' (1.5; 3.2), focuses on the threat of foreign invasion (1.5-17; 3.12-14, 16) and expresses confidence in Yahweh's help (Sweeney 2000b: 457, 479). The final verses (3.16-19) are the necessary resolution of the earlier laments (Roberts, 1991: 149). That does not mean that everything in the prayer is an original composition of the prophet. Proponents of the unity of the book accept that 3.3-15 may well utilize archaic material which circulated independently long before the time of Habakkuk. Andersen (2001: 259–61, 268) believes that 3.3-15 was an ancient poem, which was appropriated by Habakkuk to convey his message. Roberts (1991: 149) speculates that the prophet received his vision while listening to the hymn now embedded in 3.3-15.

A more detailed attempt to argue the essential connection between the prayer and the preceding material is made by Koenen. He suggests that 3.2, with its statement 'I have heard', would make an unusual opening for a psalm, but connects with 2.1 where the prophet anticipates Yahweh to speak to him. The first person singular speech in 3.2, 14-19 is a natural continuation of the first person singular in chapters one and two. The request to God to 'revive' his work 'in the midst of the years', that is, not to delay its fulfilment, flows from 2.3-4 where the anticipation of the vision's delay is expressed, and the same root *hyh* ('live/revive') is used in both places. The statement 'you came out (*ys'*) for the deliverance (*yš'*) of your people' (3.13) echoes the complaint in 1.2, 4 that Yahweh does not 'deliver' (*yš'*) and justice does not 'come out' (*ys'*). The mention of the 'poor' about to be swallowed by the wicked (3.14) reminds one of the social injustices committed in the earlier chapters, especially the motif of the wicked devouring the righteous (1.13; 2.5). Finally, the motifs of the 'house' whose foundations are 'laid bare' pick up the themes of house (2.9-10) and nakedness (2.15) from the woe oracles. On the basis of these links Koenen concludes that the whole of chapter three, with the exception of the redactional additions in 3.16b, 17, 19b, belonged to the original layer of Habakkuk (Koenen 1994: 142–6; see also Prinsloo 2001; Markl 2004).

It is, however, difficult to know how much of that repetition is due to coincidence and how much of it is by design. For example, even though the 'wicked' reappear in 3.13 their victims are described in very different terms. In 1.4, 13 the wicked target the 'righteous', whose circle by 1.15-17 is arguably widened to include 'all nations'. In 3.13-14 the victims are 'your people', 'your anointed one' (the king) and in a very difficult text 'the poor'. None of these terms harks back onto anything from the preceding chapters. The mention of the king as recipient of divine help is especially awkward if the original layer of the book attacked social injustices and the ruling class. Key concepts like 'justice' and 'violence' from chapter one are completely missing from the prayer of chapter three. Conversely, a key term like *rḡz* (agitation, trembling) which plays an important role in the prayer (3.2, 7, 16) does not appear at all in chapters one and two.

Moreover, while chapter three could very well be read as a conclusion of the book, there is some mismatch between it and chapters one and two at the level of content. The woe oracles in 2.6-20 provide a satisfying and effective conclusion (Hiebert 1986: 135). The Babylonians, whose violence is decried in 1.2-17 will be punished for their greed and oppression. The punishment is brought about by the outworking of the consequences of their wicked deeds. Shame (2.10, 16) and ridicule (2.6) play an important part in it. Nature does not feature prominently in the execution of punishment. In chapter three, on the other hand, judgement is pictured as the personal intervention of Yahweh at whose appearance creation recoils and the nations, victims in chapters one and two, but objects of wrath in chapter 3, shudder. Shame plays no role now, only sheer violence. The mythological language results in a picture that is cosmic and less tied to the more specific, historically bound imagery of 1.5–2.17. The opening request to Yahweh to 'remember mercy in anger' also does not connect well with the context. The mercy is obviously meant for his people, not for the Babylonians, but in the preceding chapters Judah is not overtly depicted as the object of Yahweh's wrath, only the 'wicked'.

The description of agricultural disaster in 3.17 takes the chapter in a completely different direction. It fits well neither with the military threat nor with the charges of oppression that are the focus of chs 1–2. These verses tie in well with 3.2-15 where the presence of the divine warrior leads to the convulsion of nature and, in keeping with its presumed cultic character, allow the prayer as a whole to apply to a variety of situations of need, both military and agricultural. In view of the more narrow focus on violence and justice in 1.2–2.16, however, their appearance at the end of chapter 3 is surprising.

Finally, chapter three has its own separate superscription (3.1), which separates it from chapters one and two. It exhibits a number of features typical of the Psalms. These include the designation 'prayer' (*tᵉp̄illāh*) in 3.1 (Psalms 17, 86, 90, 102, 142), the only three occurrences of the word *selāh* (3.3, 9, 13) outside of the Psalter, where this word appears seventy-one times, and the concluding phrase in 3.19 'to the choirmaster with stringed instruments' (Pss. 4.1; 6.1; 54.1; 55.1; 67.1). Taken together these features suggest that Habakkuk 3 once had a separate independent existence connected to the cult (Nogalski 1993b: 154–9).

Rudolph (1975: 239–40) attempts to counter the force of this evidence by pointing out that in the Psalms such features are generally recognized as later insertions and the same must also be true here (also Pfeiffer 2005: 164; Wöhrle 2008a: 322). However, if the text of chapter three existed from the start as an integral part of the preceding material, we must ask why are the liturgical insertions confined only to it? It is more plausible to assume that they fulfilled a function when the text was independently used in the cult and were retained upon its incorporation into the book of Habakkuk. In view of this, it is reasonable to conclude that the psalm existed independently and was attached secondarily to Habakkuk 1–2 (Hiebert 1986; Nogalski 1993b; Lescow 1995: 84).

Date and provenance of chapter three

According to Hiebert, the hymn preserves a pre-monarchic tradition of Yahweh being worshipped in the south, which reflects the time prior to the rise of Zion. It should be noted in passing that this thesis rests on a broader historical basis, sometimes called the Kenite hypothesis, according to which the Israelites adopted the worship of Yahweh from Kenite and Midianite tribes who lived in the south of Canaan (Albertz 1994: 51–2; Blenkinsopp 2008). The poem in Habakkuk 3 plays an important role in such reconstructions because, together with three other texts that are deemed to be very ancient as well (Judges 5; Psalms 68 and Deuteronomy 33), it attests to the existence of a motif of Yahweh's coming from the south to help his people. Building on this hypothesis Hiebert (1986: 120–4, 141) suggests that the hymn was composed and used in a Yahwistic sanctuary in the southern Transjordan from where it subsequently migrated to the Jerusalem Temple, via the north. In the post-exilic period it was attached to Habakkuk 1–2 by proto-apocalyptic groups which read the recital of the ancient acts of Yahweh eschatologically, as an expectation for the future divine intervention (1986: 136–40). As part of that process the hymn was attributed to Habakkuk, reinterpreted as prayer, and the theophany was understood as description of a visionary experience (1986: 144–9).

Nogalski (1993b: 154–81) suggests 3.2-16a, 18-19 was a self-standing composition from the late exilic period to which 3.16b-17 were added when it was integrated, together with Habakkuk 1–2, into the book of the Twelve. Anderson (2011) proposes a similar reconstruction, although he dates the two traditions in 3.3-7 and 3.8-15 to pre-monarchic times, and suggests they were combined in the pre-exilic period and then transformed into a psalm in the early Persian period by the additions of the frame (3.1-2, 16a, 18-19). Lortie (2016: 141–2, 154–61) favours an exilic dating.

Pfeiffer (2005: 151–77) argues for an original core in 3.3-12* to which 3.2a, 13-16a* were added when the text was incorporated into the book of Habakkuk. The most distinctive part of Pfeiffer's thesis is the insistence that this core contains no ancient traditions and is to be dated to the early Hellenistic period. It is an eschatological description of theophany which proclaims universal judgement of the nations, a conception that arose late and betrays familiarity with Persian royal ideology. The motif of Yahweh's coming from the south (3.3) is late (see also Pfeiffer 2017). It presupposes the existence of the judgement on Edom tradition found in Isa. 63.1-6 and the equation of Edom with the nations.

Such a late dating, however, is unconvincing. The imagery of 3.5-15 employs traditional mythological motifs (Jöcken 1977: 290–313; Day 1985: 204–9) which are not to be understood literally as depicting an apocalyptic universal judgement. The mention of the king ('the anointed one') in 3.13 makes little sense in the post-exilic period and is most naturally placed during the time of the monarchy (Seybold 1991: 47, 75, 80) when the victory of the king was equivalent to the victory of the people (contra Nogalski 1993b: 169; Perlitt 2004: 91). Moreover, nothing in the poem indicates a familiarity with, or a connection to, a 'judgement on Edom' tradition. Edom is not mentioned at all in Habakkuk 3 – Yahweh comes from Teman and Paran. In Isa. 63.1-6 Yahweh travels from one massacre to another, while in Hab. 3.3-4 Yahweh's initial appearance in the south is portrayed in an entirely positive light. It is only as Yahweh departs from the southern regions that the picture becomes more menacing. The implication of his march in 3.5-15 is that the nations that are startled and trampled upon do not live in Edom's territory.

The traditional interpretation, according to which Yahweh comes from the southern regions of Teman and Paran because he was worshipped there in pre-Israelite times and so in later periods continued to be associated with that place, has still a lot to commend it (Jeremias 2017; Leuenberger 2017). Leuenberger (2010: 4–11) points out that the name Yahweh is connected in three Late Bronze Age Egyptian texts to the southern areas of Palestine. It describes a subregion of the land of the Shasu (nomadic tribal groups) and possibly a designation of the deity worshipped by the people in that region (cf. Shupak 2001: 110). There is still some reason to believe that the Song of Deborah in Judges 5 provides us with an early attestation of an Israelite belief of Yahweh's association with that same general region (Leuenberger 2010: 11–16). The appearance of the phrase 'Yahweh of Teman' is also attested at the end of the ninth century in Kuntillet 'Ajrud and, similar to Hab. 3.3, bears testimony to a conviction about Yahweh's special association with the southern region (Emerton 1982: 10; Perlitt 2004: 86).

Conclusion

It is best to take the song in Habakkuk 3 as a pre-exilic composition which was transmitted in the cult independently of Habakkuk 1–2. It is possible that in the course of its transmission a number of glosses were added to it, expanding the possibilities of its application to agricultural crises (3.17), military attacks (3.16b) or even the Babylonian exile (see the reference to dispersing in 3.14). These broad and general descriptions of disaster suit a continued cultic use. Their language, however, betrays no conscious effort to tie in the poem to Habakkuk 1–2 or the wider book of the Twelve. The only expression that witnesses to such a desire is the addition of 'Habakkuk the prophet' to the superscription in v. 1. The hermeneutical implications of this are significant. We can read the book of Habakkuk as a unity, but we can also read chs 1–2 and ch. 3 separately from each other as independent compositions.

Further study

On Habakkuk 3 see especially the monographs of Hiebert 1986 and Lortie 2016. On the independent history of Habakkuk 3 see Hiebert 1986; Nogalski 1993b; Anderson 2011 and on its links to chapters one and two see Koenen 1994; Sweeney 2000a; Prinsloo 2001, 2002. Watts 1996 explores the conventions that govern the psalm's role in its literary context and Markl 2004 looks at its connections with the wider canonical context.

For the late dating of the chapter see Pfeiffer 2005 and Nogalski 1993b, contrast Leuenberger 2010. On the debate of the date of Yahweh's association with the south contrast Pfeiffer 2017 with Jeremias 2017 and Leuenberger 2017. On the 'Kenite hypothesis' see Albertz 1994: 51–2; Blenkinsopp 2008. On the mythological imagery see Jöcken 1977 and Day 1985. Schupak 2001 argues for possible Egyptian connections.

13

Theodicy, empire and violence: Reflections on the theology of Habakkuk

Chapter Outline

Theodicy and the final form of the book	79
Challenging empire (Habakkuk 1–2)	81
God and violence (Habakkuk 3)	82
Further study	85

Theodicy and the final form of the book

The book of Habakkuk is shaped by a clash between theology and reality. In its background lies the contradiction between Habakkuk's experience and his expectations of God. God, according to him, is holy, pure and living (1.12-13), but the prophet is faced with injustice and violence (1.2-4). Instead of intervening to save, God remains silent and aloof. In fact his actions do not solve the problem but compound it (1.5-11). The contradiction is a cause of anguish and calls for a resolution of some kind. Thus, Habakkuk attempts a theodicy, a reconciliation of the belief in the justice of God with the reality of injustice. This complex problem receives a multiplicity of treatments in the Hebrew Bible: from assertion of human freedom and responsibility for evil to falling back on divine mystery, to eschatological speculation and even recognition of a darker side of the character of God (Crenshaw 2005).

Habakkuk makes a small contribution to this larger, multifaceted enterprise. The solution is offered by means of an implied narrative, which portrays a transformation in the prophet. The indignation and frustration evident at the start of the book are replaced by the end with a confession of trust and confidence in God's ultimate intervention (2.4; 3.16-19).

Ko (2014) analyses Habakkuk in terms of its dialogue-driven plot and the main characters: the Chaldeans (the chief antagonist), Yahweh (the protagonist) and the prophet (acting as narrator). She stresses that theodicy is treated in Habakkuk not from a philosophical but from an existential perspective. There is no explanation why God allows violence to endure. The 'answer' to the prophet's complaint is to assert that God has appointed a time for judgement (2.3-5) and that the 'deed-consequence' connection, which stands at the heart of the doctrine of retribution, is still operative (2.6-20). The prophet is the perfect example of disinterested righteousness and of the general principle that the righteous person shall live by faith (2.4). He acts as a representative of his community and as a role model to be emulated by the readers of the book (Mathews 2012: 172, 180; see also Moseman 2017). Whitehead (2016) also stresses the practical and pastoral aspects of Habakkuk's approach to theodicy but argues that there is also an element of 'deferred theodicy' evident in the book's eschatological orientation. The anticipation of God's decisive intervention in the future carries with it implicitly the notion that evil and suffering must serve some mysterious divine purpose. In a similar vein, O'Neal (2007) offers a close reading of the 'canonical shape' of the text and concludes that Habakkuk aims to persuade its readers to adopt 'a divine perspective on human history as a way to endure present inequities in divine justice' and 'experience joy while enduring perceived delays in divine intervention' (2007: 148–9).

It is possible to interpret the final form in less positive ways. O'Brien (2004: 84–5) points out the tension that exists between the divine violence in chapter three and the complaints about violence in chapters one and two and the fact that the charges levelled against God are not addressed in the vision. Snyman (2003) reads the whole book as an accusation by the non-violent prophet Habakkuk of Yahweh's indifference to and use of violence. In response to the challenge (1.2–2.1) Yahweh defends his actions (2.2-20), arguing that he restores justice in the world by means of violence. The book ends with the non-violent prophet surrendering to the terrifying violence of his God (3.1-19).

Such final-form approaches provide a useful way of making sense of the prophecy. However, the construction of Habakkuk as a narrative of prophetic transformation is an act performed by the reader. Habakkuk consists of two separate texts (chs 1–2 and ch. 3) which had prior independent existence and which were combined in an almost mechanical manner to form the present book. In addition, chapters one and two originally criticized the social injustices practised by the Judean upper class before they were reworked into a condemnation of the Babylonian empire. The prophetic text is ambiguous, partly because it results from a history of redaction, application and reuse in a variety of situations. It allows, but does not demand, to be read as a developing story. The modern reader, therefore, can choose to focus not only on the finished product, read consecutively, but also on parts of the text, read atomistically.

Challenging empire (Habakkuk 1–2)

Chitsulo (2015) offers a post-colonial reading of Habakkuk. He interprets the book as a condemnation of the 'economies of extraction' in which the local Judean elite served as a proxy of the imperial powers that dominated the ANE in oppressing poor village communities. This reconstructed picture is used to challenge the socio-economic and political situation in Malawi, in which the national political elite works under the influence of Western countries and global financial institutions to extract the resources of the country, keeping the population in perpetual poverty. While one may have doubts whether this reading reflects accurately the original historical meaning of Habakkuk, it is easy to see how the redactional reincarnations of the text allow its contours to be superimposed on the situation in Malawi in the manner proposed by Chitsulo. Another attempt at a modern appropriation can be found in Gafney (2017: 117–18), who uses Habakkuk to voice a protest against those engaged in oppression and discrimination of various minority groups in Western society.

Such readings are especially appropriate if Habakkuk 1–2 is read on its own, as a text focused not on overcoming the prophet's doubts about the justice of God but on proclaiming divine judgement on the Babylonian (and Judean) imperial regime. This composition, which originated as a critique of the Judean elite and evolved into an anti-Babylonian work during the exilic period, can be used as a means of social, economic and political criticism. The first chapter condemns the injustice and violence produced by a lawless government and a greedy imperial war machine. The second chapter gives those who are on the receiving end of such exploitation hope for the future by asserting the moral rules that govern creation. Barton (2014: 94–126) highlights the existence in ancient Israel of the idea of 'moral order', which could operate via an automatic relationship between an action and its consequence (2014: 211–26). Such moral order informs the thinking behind the woe oracles of Habakkuk 2. According to it, wickedness is the mother of its own destruction. The deeds of a tyrant inevitably culminate in downfall. This is underlined by the poetic justice that characterizes each of the woe oracles. Those who get rich by unjust lending practices will be plundered by their own creditors (2.6-7). Those who get their neighbours drunk and naked will in turn be made drunk, shamed and exposed (2.15-16).

This understanding of the way the world operates is simultaneously a reflection on the nature of God and by implication suggests that God is against the practices of the ruling empire. The divine involvement with retribution is gradually unveiled. Yahweh is not mentioned in the first two woe oracles (2.6-11), but when we come across the reference to the 'cup of the right hand of Yahweh' (2.16) in the fourth we realize that it is his power, operating behind the closed curtains of history. It is, therefore, not a coincidence that the woe oracles culminate in a contrast between the lifeless and dumb idols of the nations (2.18-19) and God present in his holy temple (2.20). The holiness of God (1.13) now appears in a different light, as an active presence in the world countering evil. As Legaspi (2017) insightfully observes, the criticism of idolatry in 2.18-19 reflects back on the picture of the Babylonian empire, worshipping its own military might and political success (1.11, 16) and seeking to swallow, like Mot, the Canaanite god of the underworld, the nations of the world (2.5). The idolatry of the empire is the adoration of its oppressive, death-dealing power. Yet, its destruction is made certain by the divine holiness and is already present in the bitter fruit into which its own wicked deeds will inevitably blossom.

God and violence (Habakkuk 3)

The involvement of the reader in the construction of the theology of the book becomes even more evident in the way the theme of violence is handled. Violence is a recurring motif in Habakkuk (1.2, 3, 9; 2.8, 17). In the opening lament it is placed in opposition to law and justice, and God is seen as the answer and negation of existing human violence (Dangl 2014: 36–7). This picture, however, is not simple as God is also involved in violence. The nation he raises in 1.5-11 is a violent conqueror, and when God finally appears in person in chapter three he himself engages in acts of violence against the nations. But can violence and war be the answer to oppression and violence? (Nogalski 2011: 675–7).

Scholars respond to this problem in a number of different ways. Fretheim (2004) connects the violence of God to the concepts of sin, judgement and salvation and argues that it is a necessary divine reaction to human wickedness, an expression of God's wrath at injustice. Its ultimate goal is the end of all violence and a new creation where peace reigns. Similarly Thomas (2018: 198–9) follows Boersma in arguing that divine violence in Habakkuk is necessary because it is a means of achieving the eschatological revelation of the glory of God and so, ultimately, an expression of God's love for people.

Kamionkowski (2007) finds such an approach problematic because, by condoning divine violence, it unwittingly justifies and perpetuates human violence in the modern world. Relying on Galtung's differentiation between direct, structural and cultural violence, she argues that the prophetic imagination of divine violence is part and parcel of an overall encompassing system of violence that provides legitimation for certain structures of coercion and power (temple, monarchy, gender, circumstances of birth and so on). According to her, the task of the scholar is not to condemn the visions of violence in the biblical texts but to use those texts to unmask the cultural assumptions that blind us to acts and processes of violence in our own day.

Dempsey sees the picture of a warrior God in Habakkuk as intensely disturbing for the same reasons – it has the potential to justify the use of violence for the sake of justice. Her solution is to take this picture as an outdated reflection of the historical context of the biblical text, treat it with extreme caution and evaluate it 'in light of today's world and cultures', 'lest readers … [begin to] act as God does in the text' (2000: 85). Heard (1997) attempts to deconstruct Habakkuk, using its internal inconsistencies in order to demonstrate how the text works against its own message. He suggests that the injustice of the Chaldean violence against Judah can be used to question and undermine the justice of Yahweh's even more extreme violence against the Babylonians. He also introduces an unmentioned other in the text: the innocent Judean and Babylonian children who (presumably) suffer from the successive waves of violence in Habakkuk. Such a deconstructive reading commemorates the unnamed victims of 587 and 539 BCE and 'could thereby discourage cruelty to present and future generations of children' (1997: 87).

It is important, however, to recognize that the violent potential of the biblical text can be realized in different directions, as Klawans (2007) shows particularly well, because ultimately violence comes from the human mind and heart, not from words written on a page. A self-righteous group convinced that their enemies are evil can use the prophetic book to legitimize their own violent practices. Yet, from a position of victimhood 'a theopoetic acknowledgement of the violence of the Hidden God might indeed transform the aggressive energies of the human psyche, soul, and body into active and nonviolent expressions of peacemaking on earth' (Holland 2002: 480). The contexts within which violent texts were composed and meant to be read matters (Haak 2010). With regard to the vision of God's destructive march in Habakkuk 3, both Dangl (2014: 122–3) and Bail (2012: 448) emphasize that the prayer is uttered in the context of suffering and persecution by a prophet representing a weak and helpless community. The aggressive dimension of the picture of God is permissible in such circumstances, but only on the lips of the victim of violence, never in the mouth of the perpetrator, not as a proposed course of action but as a fantasy which helps one survive the trauma and refrain from violence in the real world.

In addition, Geller (2007) argues that the nature of the biblical text prohibits literalistic readings of the prophetic visions of violence and instead requires that these be read metaphorically. Carvalho (2010) explores what this means in relation to our understanding of the nature of God. According to her, the picture of God's violence possesses a terrifying, yet simultaneously attractive, quality because it appeals to our own penchant for violence. It is a metaphor originating from the human realm, which points to a divine reality that is 'ultimately indescribable' (2010:150). At the same time the grotesqueness of this portrayal alerts the reader that this divine behaviour, glorious and appealing as it is, is not to be imitated. Carvalho (2010: 150–1) concludes, 'I read these texts as revealing something true about God's power and sovereignty. ... I am attracted to this kind of God [because] ... I want a God who cares enough to be angry, involved enough to do something, and divine enough to accomplish what humans shouldn't even try.'

One final aspect to consider is the wider canonical context of Habakkuk 3 which contains other images and perspectives. As a religious text Habakkuk is not meant to be read in isolation but as part of a broader tradition that interprets it and places constrains on the direction of its application. Claassens (2012, 2016) emphasizes three marginal metaphors for God in the Hebrew Bible that should, in her view, play a crucial role in contemporary theological discourse. God is portrayed as a mourning woman in Jeremiah, as a mother in Isaiah and as a midwife in the Psalms. These metaphors convey the sense of God's 'incarnational' presence in human suffering and picture a non-violent, life-giving deliverer qualitatively different from the image of a destructive warrior God that dominates the tradition. Claassens acknowledges that these metaphors are peripheral but argues that they should be given prominence because they 'complicate', 'challenge', 'balance' and 'enrich' the prevalent understanding of a violent and distant deity.

In my view, Claassens proposal provides a helpful addition to and qualification of Carvalho's approach. Theologically Habakkuk 3 cannot be rejected or ignored. The violence of God is necessary, terrifying and glorious, as Carvalho shows well. At the same time Habakkuk 3 cannot be read in isolation. It needs to be seen in conjunction with those other strands of tradition that depict a different side to divine reality. From a distinctly Christian point of view, Thomas (2018: 199–202), relying on the work of Girard, points out that in Christ God overcomes violence by siding with the victims of violence and becoming a victim of abuse. This must be the central vantage point from which the vision of Habakkuk is understood.

Ultimately, the theology of Habakkuk will always depend on the way its readers choose to interact with the text out of their current circumstances and on the basis of their prior ethical and theological convictions, political views and cultural expectations. Those who seek justification for their violence will always be able to find it. A moral responsibility rests on the shoulders of the reader.

Further study

Mathews 2012 offers a final-form reading of Habakkuk from the perspective of performance criticism. For Habakkuk as a story of the transformation of the prophet which the reader is to imitate see Moseman 2017. O'Neal 2007 offers a canonical reading of the book, while Ko 2014 and Whitehead 2016 explore more specifically the issue of theodicy in it. On theodicy in the Hebrew Bible consult Crenshaw 2005. For a post-colonial reading of Habakkuk see Chitsulo 2015. An excellent discussion of 'moral order' in the Hebrew Bible can be found in Barton 2014. Imperial idolatry in Habakkuk is discussed by Legaspi 2017.

On God and violence in Habakkuk see Heard 1997; Snyman 2003; O'Brien 2004; Nogalski 2011; Bail 2012; Dangl 2014; Dietrich 2016; Thomas 2018. More generally on the issue of divine violence in the Hebrew Bible see Bernat and Klawans 2007; O'Brien and Franke 2010; Zehnder and Hagelia 2013 and especially the contrasting perspectives of Fretheim 2004; Klawans 2007; Kamionkowski 2007; Carvalho 2010 and Claassens 2012, 2016. See also the survey in Jones 2016.

Part Four

Zephaniah

14 The genre and structures of the
    book of Zephaniah

15 Zephaniah the prophet

16 Zephaniah's oracles against the
    nations and the composition of 1.1–3.8

17 Zephaniah's message of hope (3.9-20)
    and the canonical shape of the book

14

The genre and structures of the book of Zephaniah

Chapter Outline

The genre of the book of Zephaniah	89
The structures of the book	92
Conclusion	95
Further study	95

The book of Zephaniah is aptly described by Mason (1994: 16) as 'the prophetic corpus in miniature'. Within its three brief chapters we encounter most of the themes and literary forms characteristic of the prophetic literature. Zephaniah proclaims judgement on the inhabitants of Judah and Jerusalem because of their cultic misdeeds and social injustice (1.2-18; 3.1-5). He calls the nation to repent and seek Yahweh (2.1-3; 3.6-8) in the hope of escaping the devastation of the Day of the Lord (1.14-16). The prophet announces judgement of a number of foreign nations (2.4-15). Finally, he proclaims salvation for the nations (3.9-10), for the remnant of the people (3.11-13) and the restoration of Zion (3.14-20).

The genre of the book of Zephaniah

In order to understand Zephaniah it is imperative to have some idea about what kind of text we are reading and what we should expect from it. House (1989) suggests that the book is a prophetic drama, structured around a dialogue between two speakers, Yahweh and the prophet. This proposal is often quoted but rarely accepted by scholars (see the criticisms of Roberts 1991: 161 and O'Brien 2004: 87). During most of the twentieth century interpreters have treated Zephaniah primarily as a compilation of prophetic oracles which was subsequently developed by means of glosses and additions (see, for example, Lindblom 1967: 220–2, 252–3). In recent times this approach has not been entirely abandoned but has been significantly modified. Modern scholarship tends to emphasize more strongly the scribal, reinterpretative character of the written prophetic word (Kratz 2015a: 31–2, 101–4). In addition, the attention has shifted away from the initial stages of the putative collection of revelations and towards the nature of the finished literary product that is the prophetic book.

Sweeney (1991b) argues that Zephaniah as a whole is best described as a 'prophetic exhortation' in which the announcement of the Day of the Lord in chapter one serves to motivate the call to seek God in chapters two and three. Floyd (2000: 171–3) agrees partially with this proposal but points out that it does not take into account the superscription. The opening verse talks about Zephaniah in the third person and looks back on his ministry from the perspective of a later time. It implies that the author is an anonymous scribe who presents to his readership the preaching of a prophet of old. The book, therefore, is 'prophetic instruction' in which the author uses the prophecy of Zephaniah for the purposes of theological education of his audience.

In fact, Floyd (2006) argues that the genre of the prophetic book as we know it emerged with the Babylonian exile as a result of the changes in Israel's world view and divinatory practices following this traumatic experience (see also Nissinen 2017: 151–2). For him the assumption of the mantle of a prophetic character from the past by an anonymous scribal author along with the reinterpretation of prophetic tradition and the rhetoric of exhortation are defining features of the genre of the prophetic book. In a similar vein Stulman (2007) describes written prophecy as 'survival literature' and Ben Zvi (2009a) thinks the genre of prophetic books functioned as means of shaping the identity of the community in the Persian period by preserving the memories of the past and offering hope for the future.

In a complete break from the traditional approach Mack (2011) suggests that Zephaniah be regarded as a purely literary composition which does not rely on any pre-existing oracular material. It simply utilizes and transforms known older genres, not older prophetic collections. A connection, which Mack does not make but scholars have claimed for other prophetic books, can arguably be established with a group of Mesopotamian works called 'literary-predictive texts' (Radine 2010: 110–23; contrast Grund 2013: 242–3). These compositions contain descriptions of political events, fictitiously cast as prediction, with the aim of serving a political agenda, namely legitimizing the reign of a certain king. They are literary compositions right from the start and have no connection to prior oral prophetic proclamation (De Jong 2007: 420–37). While the movement from a period of chaos and disaster to a time of salvation connects literary-predictive texts and the book of Zephaniah, there are also important differences both in terms of literary shape and sociological function. Moreover, literary-critical study of Zephaniah still shows traces of the earlier collections of prophetic material, as will be shown below (pp. 92–95, 99–102).

In that sense Zephaniah, not in its finished form but certainly in some of its earlier iterations, also bears a certain resemblance to literary elaborations of oral prophecy in Assyria, of which SAA 9.9 provides a good example (for the text see Parpola 1997: 40–1; Nissinen 2003: 130–1). That text is based on a prophecy originally delivered in 650 BCE during the war between Ashurbanipal and his brother Shamash-shum-ukin, but in its current shape it was probably written after Shamash-shum-ukin's death in 648 BCE. The oracle contains a number of allusions to the Gilgamesh epic (Parpola 1997: 41 n. 8–15). The literary reworking preserves the perspective of the original oracle but enhances its rhetorical power and generalizes its meaning (De Jong 2007: 405–8). Both literary-predictive texts and literary elaborations of prophetic oracles from Mesopotamia bear some resemblance to Zephaniah but do not provide a close enough parallel to it in terms of genre.

A helpful conceptual basis for understanding the nature of the book is offered by Lange (2006) who makes an important distinction between 'written' and 'literary' prophecy. According to him, written prophecies either serve archival purposes or help bridge a geographical communication gap; that is, the addressee of the oracle is not physically present at the time of its delivery and the message needs to be given in written form in order for it to reach them. Literary prophecy, on the other hand, is designed to bridge a much bigger chronological communication gap – it is addressed to future generations. The key difference between these two kinds of prophecy comes from the process of reapplication of the prophetic word which is evident in literary prophecy. Written prophecy, even when it is recorded for archival purposes, preserves in essence its original meaning. In contrast, literary prophecy is placed in a new context, connected to the experience of a new generation of readers and so reapplied to meet the needs of the new situation (see also Nissinen 2000: 263–8). It has a 'surplus of meaning', which was not present there at the start but emerges through the process of recontextualization.

In Lange's terms Zephaniah is best described as a literary prophecy, that is, the reapplication of the tradition of the prophet to a later exilic and post-exilic situation by several generations of readers and redactors. The message originates in a defined historical situation but transcends that situation to address the future. Literary prophecy is multi-layered and needs to be read with several successive historical contexts simultaneously operating in the background.

The structures of the book

The book of Zephaniah is often analysed in terms of a tripartite structure (Boadt 1982: 207; Ben Zvi 1991: 325–6; Perlitt 2004: 98)

   I. Oracles of judgement against Judah and Jerusalem (1.2–2.3)
  II. Oracles against foreign nations (2.4-15)
 III. Oracles of restoration and salvation (3.1-20).

The books of Isaiah, Ezekiel and LXX Jeremiah exhibit a similar arrangement, and so Zephaniah is deemed to follow a well-recognized pattern. According to Ben Zvi (1991), this common pattern is so significant that it holds the key to understanding the overall message of the book and its historical situation (see below p. 98). In this model the judgement on the foreign enemy nations, following on from the announcement of judgement upon Judah, serves as a prelude to the proclamation of the salvation of Judah.

The problem with place and role of 3.1-8

The neat tripartite scheme, however, is disturbed by the presence of an oracle of judgement against Jerusalem in 3.1-8. This oracle serves as the climax of the preceding OAN and prevents the reader from seeing the judgement on Judah's neighbours as a simple prelude to the salvation of Judah. Its position at the end of the series of OAN, the repetition in 3.8 of the refrain from 1.18 and the accusation that the soiled and oppressive city has not accepted correction (3.2, 7), all create the impression that Jerusalem's judgement must be seen as part and parcel of the punishment of the nations of the world (Ryou 1995: 325–6). This insight is reflected in Gorgulho's structural proposal (1991: 90–1):

    I.   The coming of the Day of Yahweh (1.1-18)
    II. Return and judgement (2.1–3.5)
    III. The project for the future (3.6-20)

This structure, however, is not without its problems, because two of the OAN also contain a different perspective on the themes of judgement and salvation. In 2.7 and 2.9b-10 the demise of the Philistines, Ammonites and Moabites leads directly to benefits for the people of Yahweh who inherit their territories. There is, therefore, an inherent ambiguity in the text of Zephaniah 2. The destruction of the foreign nations is simultaneously a prelude to Judah's judgement and to the salvation of the remnant of Judah surviving that judgement.

The problem with unity of 3.9-20 and its connection to the OAN

The ending of the book (3.9-20) is superficially unified by the theme of salvation. Because of this Vlaardingerbroeck (1999: 9–10; see also Dietrich 2016) treats the salvation material in 3.9-20 as the last major section of the book:

    I.   The Day of the Lord against Judah and Jerusalem (1.2–2.3)
    II.   Against peoples small and great (2.4-15)
    III. Against Jerusalem (3.1-8)
    IV. Salvation after Judgement (3.9-20)

However, the subsections of this passage focus on different groups as recipients of Yahweh's beneficial actions: the nations (3.9-10), the remnant (3.11-13), Zion (3.14-20). These subsections are juxtaposed without any other obvious links between them and at the same time they connect thematically to some of the earlier oracles. Both the salvation of the nations (3.9-10) and of the remnant (3.11-13) passages point to different strands in the OAN (2.4-15) and so could legitimately be seen as the continuation and conclusion of that whole section, rather than as an introduction to the following 3.14-20. Therefore, O'Brien (2004: 90–1) takes 3.9-13 as part of the Jerusalem oracle and sees the decisive break in 3.14 with its change to direct address. This results in the following structure for Zephaniah:

    I.   Coming punishment (1.2-18)
   II.   Call to repentance (2.1-3[4])
  III.   Judgement on the nations (2.5-15)
  IV.   Woe and salvation to Judah (and the nations) (3.1-13)
   V.   Promises of restoration for Judah (and the nations) (3.14-20)

Similarly, Floyd (2000: 165–6), who builds on the work of Sweeney (1991b), offers the following arrangement:

    I.   Announcement of the Day of Yahweh (1.2-18)
   II.   Exhortation to prepare for the Day of Yahweh (2.1–3.13)
  III.   Exhortation to rejoice in the promise of salvation (3.14-20)

The problem with place and role of 2.1-3

When one compares the proposals of Vlaardingerbroek, O'Brien and Floyd, another odd feature of Zephaniah's literary arrangement becomes apparent – the place of 2.1-3 within the structure. Vlaardingerbroek takes it as the conclusion of chapter one, Sweeney and Floyd as the opening of the second part and O'Brien treats it as a separate passage. On the one hand, 2.1-3 is thematically related to the oracles in chapter one. The 'day of Yahweh's anger' in 2.2-3 recalls the 'day of the Lord' passage in 1.14-16 and alludes to the 'day of the Lord's fury' in 1.18. The invitation to *seek* Yahweh builds on the accusation in 1.6. Yet, formally the passage is separated from 1.2-18 and belongs with the following OAN. The refrain in 1.18 (repeated in 3.8), whose universal perspective parallels 1.2-3, seems to function as a concluding statement to the oracles in chapter one, while the imperatives of 2.1 indicate the beginning of a new section. Conversely, there is no formal break between 2.3 and the following verse. Instead, the opening 'because' of 2.4 invites the reader to see it as a continuation of the preceding. In this case formal and thematic criteria point in opposite directions (Hadjiev 2014: 511). Within the larger structure of the book 2.1-3 parallels 3.6-8, the other passage that discusses the topic of repentance. Ryou's (1995: 282) proposed chiastic structure brings out this parallel:

A The Day of Yahweh coming on Judah and Jerusalem (1.2-18)

    B Call to repentance (2.1-4)

        C Oracles against the nations (2.5–3.5)

    B' Refusal to repent (3.6-8)

A' Redemption of the remnant (3.9-20)

Conclusion

The reason why the short text of Zephaniah can be analysed in such a bewildering variety of ways lies in the history of its composition. Different structures reflect different stages of development of the text. It is probable that the first written composition encompassed 1.1–2.3 to which at a later stage 2.4–3.8 were added (Hadjiev 2014: 509–12). This explains why 2.1-3 looks, on the one hand, like a conclusion to the preceding (this was its original function within 1.1–2.3) and simultaneously like an introduction to the following. (This was the role created for it by the redactor who added 2.4–3.8.) In a similar manner the odd function of the OAN as announcing both the judgement of Judah in 3.1-5 and the salvation of the remnant in 3.11-13 reflects different redactional stages (Hadjiev 2011). The compiler responsible for 1.1–3.8 used the series to lead up to the climactic announcement of judgement for Jerusalem in 3.1-8. Later on the redactor who added 3.11-13 as a new conclusion to the composition reinterpreted the OAN in the more traditional sense of proclamation of Judah's restoration, by inserting 2.7, 9b-10. This redactional history and the resultant multifaceted nature of the book of Zephaniah mean that the modern reader may approach the text from a number of different perspectives. Different readers will perceive different structures and different thematic emphases because all of those are present beneath the surface of the final form of the text.

Further study

On the genre of Zephaniah consult Sweeney 1991b; Floyd 2000; Mack 2011. On Zephaniah as prophetic drama see House 1989 and contrast Roberts

1991; O'Brien 2004. On the genre of prophetic books more generally see Lange 2006; Floyd 2006; Stulman 2007; Ben Zvi 2009a; Kratz 2015a; Nissinen 2017. On Neo-Assyrian prophecy in addition to Parpola 1997 and Nissinen 2003 see also De Jong 2007; Stökl 2012; Grund 2013; Nissinen 2017. On literary-predictive texts see De Jong 2007; Radine 2010.

For the structure of Zephaniah see the discussions and different proposals of Sweeney 1991b; Ben Zvi 1991; Weigl 1994; Berlin 1994; Ryou 1995; Floyd 2000; O'Brien 2004; Hadjiev 2014.

15

Zephaniah the prophet

Chapter Outline

Can we know anything about the historical prophet?	98
Going back in time: The earlier stages of the Zephaniah tradition	99
The first Zephaniah scroll (1.1–2.3)	100
The date and profile of Zephaniah's activity	103
A black person of royal descent?	105
Further study	105

The superscription of Zephaniah makes the prophet a contemporary of King Josiah of Judah (640–609 BCE) whose reign coincided with the last days of the Assyrian Empire and the rise of Babylon. After the death of the Assyrian king Ashurbanipal (627 BCE) and the capture of Babylon by the Chaldean chief Nabopolasar (626 BCE), Assyria began to lose ground against the onslaught of the Babylonians and their allies. Ashur fell in 614 BCE, Nineveh in 612 BCE and finally Haran in 610 BCE, spelling the end of the Assyrian domination in the region. Historians debate whether with the decline of Assyria Josiah became an Egyptian vassal or managed to establish independence and enlarge the territories of his kingdom (Na'aman 2007).

Biblical tradition credits Josiah with a most radical and thoroughgoing religious reform (Albertz 2007; Uehlinger 2007) which saw the abolition of foreign cults, destruction of the altar at Bethel, renewal of the covenant and centralization of Yahwistic worship in the temple of Jerusalem (1 Kings 22–23). During the reform the 'book of the law', which is generally identified with an earlier version of the book of Deuteronomy, was found in the temple and provided further stimulus to the reforms. Biblical scholarship has credited the reign of Josiah with a number of literary achievements. Many believe that under him the first edition of the Deuteronomistic History (Deuteronomy–2 Kings) was produced, and some prophetic books underwent significant redactions (Sweeney 2001).

Can we know anything about the historical prophet?

Most scholars take the superscription at face value and thus locate Zephaniah during Josiah's reign. Ben Zvi (1996b), however, argues that such information should not be accepted uncritically as a starting point of historical investigation. Moreover, he points out that Josiah is not a major character in the book and his reform is not explicitly mentioned in the prophecy (Ben Zvi 2007). Instead, we should begin with the tripartite structure of the book, which moves from judgement on Judah to judgement on the foreign nations, to restoration (Ben Zvi 1991). The historical situation of the community which produced Zephaniah, in Ben Zvi's opinion, is the second stage of the development of the book's overall scenario: Judah has already experienced judgement; it is currently under foreign domination, and salvation is still to come. Zephaniah, therefore, explains the past disaster as divine judgement and simultaneously provides hope. It achieves that by claiming to impart secret knowledge about Yahweh's will, nature and future plans. The anonymous authors of the book create a fictitious image of the prophet Zephaniah, a recipient of divine revelation in the distant past and a sophisticated speaker who transmits that secret knowledge to his audience. This portrayal of the prophet differs radically from what real-life prophets would have been in the monarchic period and is patterned on the image of the anonymous authors of the book. By means of such rhetorical strategy they seek to delegitimize contemporary rival groups claiming prophetic inspiration and to establish their own social and religious authority in the post-monarchic community.

Similar is the approach of Mack (2011). He also dismisses the superscription's historical reliability and takes it as a rhetorical device aimed at inspiring reverence (2011: 287). The oracles do not reflect royal concerns but betray an ideological stance which makes more sense in a later period when the Davidic monarchy was seen to have failed in its duty to maintain cosmic order. The doubts about Yahweh's ability to act (1.12) also fit better in the situation after 587 BCE (2011: 295, 312–21).

Levin (2011a) also severs the connection of the book with the original proclamation of a historical prophet, but arrives at this conclusion via a different route. According to him the origin of the Zephaniah tradition is non-prophetic. The core of the book was a liturgical piece (1.7, 14-16*) which consisted of a cultic proclamation for the celebration of the Day of the Lord. This was subsequently reinterpreted as a prophecy of doom, and the book grew gradually around it by a long process of redactional additions.

Going back in time: The earlier stages of the Zephaniah tradition

Most scholars would agree that the book of Zephaniah in its finished form is a post-exilic work. However, many scholars still believe that the book is anchored in the ministry of a historical prophet from pre-exilic times. This position is based on the conviction that we can still discern within the current shape of the final text some of the earlier stages of the book's evolution. Redaction critics identify either 1.1–3.13* (Krinetzki 1977: 223–32; Ryou 1995: 310–1) or 1.1–3.10* (Seybold 1991: 85–6), or 1.1–3.8* (Neef 1999: 544–5; Striek 1999: 221–6; Irsigler 2002: 60–1; Schwesig 2006: 42–4; Hadjiev 2014: 509–12; Dietrich 2016: 189) as an early edition of Zephaniah. Of the various proposals 1.1–3.8 has the most to commend it. It looks like an independent composition in its own right, with a character, structure and theme of its own.

I.   Yahweh's cosmic judgement overtakes sinful Judah and Jerusalem (1.2-18)

Cosmic judgement (1.2-3)

The sins of Judah and Jerusalem and the coming Day of the Lord (1.4-16)

Cosmic judgement (1.17-18)
refrain: 'in the fire of his jealousy the whole earth will be devoured' (1.18)

II. Yahweh's judgement against foreign nations overtakes unrepentant Judah and Jerusalem (2.1–3.8)

Call to seek Yahweh (2.1-3)

Against the Philistines (2.4-6)
Against Moab and the Ammonites (2.8-9a)
Against Cush (2.12)
Against Assyria (2.13-15)
Against Jerusalem (3.1-5)

Cosmic judgement and a call to wait for Yahweh (3.6-8)
refrain: 'in the fire of his jealousy the whole earth will be devoured' (3.8)

The text revolves around the theme of disaster that has engulfed the whole world and is now threatening Judah. The day of Yahweh's anger was provoked by the sins of Jerusalem's elite (1.4-16) and it can be avoided only by turning to Yahweh (2.1-3). The final three verses (3.6-8) provide this composition with a fitting conclusion. They summarize the theme of world judgement, echoing the language of the preceding sections ('without inhabitant' from 2.5; 'punish/visit' from 1.8, 9, 12; 'gather' from 1.2-3; 'the fury of my wrath' from 2.2), and restate the call to seek Yahweh from 2.1-3 in terms of 'waiting' for his *day* (see 1.14-16) when he will 'rise to plunder'.

The first Zephaniah scroll (1.1–2.3)

Even though 1.1–3.8 is unified structurally and thematically, it does not read like a piece cut out of a single cloth. For one, Zephaniah 2.4–3.5 looks very much like a collection of pre-existing materials. Unlike Amos 1.3–2.16, Zephaniah's OAN have no regularity or uniformity. They vary in length and structure and contain neither repeating formulas nor common patterns. In contrast, 1.1–2.3 is held together by its own thematic development and structure. It revolves around the concept of the day of the Lord's anger, a concept entirely missing from 2.4–3.5. The call to seek Yahweh in order to avert the consequences of divine anger (2.1-3) serves well as the climax and conclusion of this composition. On purely literary-critical grounds, therefore, 1.1–2.3 seems to form a core (Vlaardingerbroek 1999: 25; Hadjiev 2014: 512–16) which at a subsequent stage was expanded by the addition of various, originally independent, oracles against foreign nations (2.4-15), with 3.6-8 composed to serve as its new conclusion.

This text has the character of a literary composition. In the opening passage (1.2-3) almost everything is repeated twice, or comes in pairs, except the Hebrew verb 'I will sweep away' (the form and meaning of this verb is disputed, see Vlaardingerbroek 1999: 57–9) which is used three times:

(i) Sweeping (ii) *I will sweep away* all from upon the face of the earth, says Yahweh.
I will sweep away (i) humans and (ii) beasts.
I will sweep away (i) the birds of the heavens and (ii) the fish of the sea.
and I will cut off the humans from upon the face of the earth, says Yahweh.

This pattern of repetition is central to the whole of 1.2–2.3 and shows that vv. 2-3 were composed as its introduction. The twofold repetition is most visible in the little poem of 1.15-16 which follows the model established in 1.3 (every line begins with the same word followed by a pair of parallel terms):

A (i) *day* of anger is that (ii) *day*
a *day* of (i) distress and (ii) trouble
a *day* of (i) desolation and (ii) devastation
a *day* of (i) darkness and (ii) gloom
a *day* of (i) cloud and (ii) mist
a *day* of (i) trumpet and (ii) cry
against the (i) cities, the (ii) fortified (ones)
and against the (i) towers, the (ii) lofty (ones).

Twofold repetition also plays a structuring role within the composition as a whole. The text begins and ends with two phrases consisting of two words which either derive from the same root or at least sound as if they do: 'sweeping I will sweep away' (*ʾāsōp̄ ʾāsēp̄*) (1.2) and 'gather yourselves like stubble and gather stubble' (*hiṯqôšᵉšû wāqōššû*) (2.1). The twice repeated phrase 'the Day of the Lord is near' (1.7, 14) splits the first chapter in three parts of roughly equal length. At the very end the phrase 'the day of the wrath of the Lord' is repeated twice (2.2, 3).

The threefold repetition of the verb 'I will sweep away' in 1.2-3 sets the stage for another pattern of repetition in 1.4–2.3, where several key words occur three times in all: 'human beings' (*ʾāḏām*) 1.3 (×2), 17; 'inhabitants' 1.4, 11, 18; 'and I will punish' (*ûp̄āqaḏtî*) 1.8, 9, 12. This is most visible in the concluding passage (2.1-3) where the words 'before', 'seek', 'day' and the phrase 'the wrath of the Lord' all come up three times in the short space of three verses. Complex wordplays and allusions to other prophetic texts also point to the literary nature of this composition. The ambiguous phrase *lōʾ*

nikṣāp in 2.1, which could be translated not only as 'who have no shame'/'who are not desired' but also as 'who have no silver', clearly plays on the double mention of the word 'silver' (*kesep*) in the description of Judean sin (1.11) and punishment (1.18). The Day of the Lord passage (1.14-16), and especially the conditional promise of rescue, introduced with 'perhaps' (*'ûlay*) in 2.3, are generally recognized as influenced by Amos 5.14-15 and 5.18-20.

Many interpreters consider the universalistic language of 1.2-3 and 1.18* as a 'proto-apocalyptic' description of eschatological events. For this reason the verses are regarded either as additions or as an indication that the whole chapter is to be dated late (Hagedorn 2011b: 463). This view, however, is based on an unduly literalistic reading of the text. The cosmic flavour of the disaster is nothing more than a rhetorical device. The coming punishment of Judah is depicted as if it were the end of the world in order to underscore the severity of the situation. There is no need to read into it an expectation of a literal apocalypse (Hadjiev 2014: 513–15).

The section that deals with Judah's cultic offences (1.4-6) has a number of links to the description of Josiah's reforms in 2 Kings 23. The mention of Baal (2 Kgs 23.4, 5), the idolatrous priests (2 Kgs 23.5), worship on the roofs (2 Kgs 23.12) and the host of heaven (2 Kgs 23.4, 5) connects these passages. Some, therefore, believe Zeph. 1.4-6 is a later deuteronomistic addition, influenced by the text of Kings. However, the two texts are sufficiently different to preclude any direct literary relationship (Hadjiev 2010: 327). The references in Zephaniah are more likely reminiscences of the historical situation prior to, or during, the reforms.

The cultic and social criticisms of chapter one fit well in the general period of Josiah. The composition does not condemn discrete groups of people, but the Judean elite as a whole. These people benefitted economically from the integration of Judah in the Assyrian Empire and were influenced by foreign customs and religious practice. The references to astral worship and foreign priests (1.4-5), and the condemnation of those who wear foreign attire (1.8) point to the cosmopolitan nature of the life of Judean aristocracy resulting from imperial Assyrian influence (Cogan 1974: 88–96; Uehlinger 1996; Striek 1999: 219–20). It is possible that this text was produced by scribes at Josiah's court in order to support the king's religious reforms. Its parenetic nature, evident in the climactic exhortation to seek Yahweh (2.1-3) motivated by the preceding criticisms and threats (1.2-18), suggests that it was composed in order to persuade and influence behaviour. Its rhetoric suggests that the support for the reforms was billed as equivalent to an authentic return to Yahweh, practice of justice and renouncing of corrupt foreign ways.

Can we go behind this original written tradition to reconstruct the ministry of the historical prophet Zephaniah? The high degree of literary artistry of 1.1–2.3 suggests that, not unlike SAA 9.9 mentioned above, we are faced here with a literary elaboration of a collection of prophetic oracles, not simply with a mechanical transcript of their oral delivery. The question is whether this literary elaboration has any connection to an actual prophetic message proclaimed orally prior to it. The truth of the matter is that we have no way of knowing for certain. Many scholars are sceptical that we can penetrate the 'scribal filter' of reinterpretation through which the words of the prophets come to us (Nissinen 2000: 244–5, 2017: 146–50; Stökl 2012: 132, 137, 219; Kratz 2015a: 27, 33; cf. Van der Toorn 2000: 230–3). Others think that the prophets in the late monarchical period developed a 'scribal mentality' and thought it important to write down their revelations out of concern for their preservation and the protection of their immutability (Schaper 2005), or as a primary means of dissemination of the message (Floyd 1993). Some think this was true of Zephaniah in particular who was responsible for the first written composition of his preaching (Striek 1999: 227–33; Albertz 2003a: 220 n. 251). Vlaardingerbroek (1999: 25) is of the opinion that 'the literary form and the redactional structure of (esp.) 1.2–2.3 make it unlikely that oral preaching lay behind this material. … Zephaniah's prophetic ministry only took place in written form'.

The date and profile of Zephaniah's activity

Among those who think they can reconstruct Zephaniah's message behind the first written script there is a great deal of variety concerning the contents and shape of that message. Hagedorn (2011a: 113–20, 124–9, 2011b) discerns only one original Zephaniah oracle directed against Philistia, Moab and Ammon and prefixed by the Day of the Lord saying (1.14b-16 + 2.4-5, 8-9). Kratz (2015a: 55) restricts the original oracle to 1.14-16. Most scholars are more generous and believe that at least parts of chapter one reflect the oral preaching of Zephaniah. Perlitt (2004: 98), who still represents a minimalist position, identifies a collection of prophetic oracles in 1.4-16. Albertz (2003a: 220 n.251) thinks that after 604 BCE Zephaniah himself composed 1.7–2.4* on the basis of some of his earlier oracles. Irsigler (2002: 59–60) and Dietrich (2016: 188), in addition to most of the material in chapter one, include some OAN and 3.1-4*. The OAN will be addressed in the next chapter.

Most scholars date Zephaniah's activity to the early part of Josiah's reign (c. 630 BCE), before the famous reforms of 2 Kings 22–23 began in 622 BCE (Fohrer 1974: 13; Kapelrud 1975: 42; Roberts, 1991: 163–4; Blenkinsopp 1996: 113–15; Neef 1999: 544; Irsigler 2002: 67–9; Perlitt 2004: 97; Dietrich 2016: 188). The suggestions to place the prophet in the later part of Josiah's reign, c. 615 BCE (Seybold 1991: 88), or during the reign of Jehoiakim, 609–597 BCE (Hyatt 1948; Williams 1963; Nogalski 1993a: 179–80), have not attracted wide following.

The nature of Zephaniah's relationship to the Jerusalem establishment is estimated differently. According to Sweeney (2003a: 14–18) the whole book is a scribal transcript of a public speech given by the prophet in the Jerusalem Temple. This speech was aimed at supporting the king's policies in the early stages of the reform, prior to the discovery of the law book. Hagedorn (2011b) thinks that Zephaniah supported Josiah's bid to assert his independence and was no different to his ANE colleagues whose proclamation legitimized royal policy.

Others imagine the prophet working at some distance from the establishment. Seybold (1985) suggests Zephaniah was a satirical poet critical of the court. He notes the lack of Zion and Davidic ideology in the prophecy and argues that even the fragments of the OAN that come from him are ironic criticism of Judean triumphalism, rather than genuine support for expansionist royal policy. According to Irsigler (2002: 70–1) Zephaniah was not a partisan supporter of Josiah's reforms, although his preaching may have contributed to and inspired the reform movement. Rather, Zephaniah confronted the leading circles of Jerusalem with the consequences of their social and cultic misdeeds. Following in the footsteps of Amos (5.18-20) and Isaiah (2.12-17), he proclaimed the inevitable arrival of the day of Yahweh's wrath and judgement. A similar position is adopted by Dietrich (2016: 188–9).

Vlaardingerbroek (1999: 17–25, 126–31) strikes a middle course. Zephaniah began his career supporting Josiah's reforms. This can be seen in the OAN (2.4-15) which cheer Judean ambitions for territorial expansion and rejection of Assyrian and Egyptian power. Later on, perhaps due to disillusionment, Zephaniah changed his stance and aligned himself with the 'prophetic school' that was sceptical of the royal nationalistic agenda that drove the reforms and believed in transformation through judgement. This is reflected in the darker, uncompromising message of inevitable judgement that dominates 1.2–2.3.

If the suggestion, made above, that 1.1–2.3 was composed by royal scribes in support of Josiah's policy is correct, then it is much more likely that Zephaniah was supportive of the royal court rather than fundamentally opposed to it. Any proclamation of disaster must be seen in this context as a rhetorical device aimed at motivating a certain type of behaviour, rather than as the announcement of unavoidable doom (Striek 1999: 80). Whether Zephaniah was also a scribe, involved in the writing of his own oracles, and whether the literary composition reflected the thrust of his earlier oral proclamation, or altered it significantly, is impossible to tell.

A black person of royal descent?

The book of Zephaniah is unusual in that the superscription provides a very long genealogy for the prophet that goes back four generations. Two items from that genealogy have attracted much attention. The first is Hezekiah, the great-grandfather of the prophet. If he is identical to the Judean king of the same name (2 Kings 18–20), then Zephaniah must have been a member of the royal household (Rice 1979; Gafney 2017: 134–8). The other item of interest is the name of Zephaniah's father, Cushi, meaning 'Ethiopian', which suggests that the prophet may have had African roots. Rice (1979) and Gafney (2017: 129–33) argue that Zephaniah's grandmother was Ethiopian, and her son was called Cushi to reflect her Ethiopian ancestry.

Further study

On Zephaniah as a post-exilic work not related to the figure of a historical prophet see Ben Zvi 1991; Mack 2011; Levin 2011a.

On Zephaniah and the reign of Josiah consult the various approaches by Seybold 1985; Uehlinger 1996; Vlaardingerbroek 1999; Sweeney 2003a; Ben Zvi 2007; Hagedorn 2011b; Dietrich 2016. On the reign and reforms of Josiah compare the contributions of Albertz, Uehlinger, Davis and Na'aman in Grabbe 2007. Sweeney 2001 thinks a number of historical and prophetic traditions were redacted during his reign. On dating Zephaniah during the reign of Jehoiakim see Hyatt 1948; Williams 1963; Nogalski 1993a.

On the material which is to be attributed to the prophet contrast the positions of Kapelrud 1975 and Sweeney 2003a with those of Albertz 2003a;

Perlitt 2004; Hagedorn 2011a, 2011b; Kratz 2015a and see the mediating views of Irsigler 2002, Dietrich 2016 and also of Vlaardingerbroek 1999. On the relationship between oral and written prophecy see Floyd 1993; Nissinen 2000; Van der Toorn 2000; Schaper 2005; Stökl 2012. For the redaction history of the book see also Krinetzki 1977; Striek 1999; Neef 1999; Hadjiev 2014.

On Zephaniah's possible royal and African roots see Rice 1979; Gafney 2017.

16

Zephaniah's oracles against the nations and the composition of 1.1–3.8

Chapter Outline

The shape of the OAN	107
The provenance of the OAN	108
Zephaniah 1.1–3.8 and the Babylonian exile	110
Zephaniah 1.1–3.8 and the Judean politics in the late monarchic period	112
Further study	113

The shape of the OAN

Rudolph (1975: 279) suggests that 2.4-15 is a unified composition, consisting of four oracles about five nations. The diverse literary shape of the OAN, however, make it more probable that they existed independently prior to their incorporation into the book (Roberts 1991: 195). The resultant composition is not a random collection of material but a carefully planned literary work. The nations are arranged in a geographical pattern: west (Philistia), east (Moab and Ammon), south (Cush), north (Assyria), which suggests that together they are meant to convey a sense of totality and perhaps serve as representatives of all the nations of the world. The selection of small neighbouring nations alongside more distant and powerful ones points in the same direction. The series makes little sense on its own and was likely composed right from the start as a continuation of 1.1–2.3. The opening 'because' of 2.4 creates a smooth transition between the call to seek Yahweh in 2.1-3 and the following picture of wholesale destruction. The universal devastation of the nations and Judah provides an additional motivation to heed that call in 2.3.

Like 1.1–2.3, the addition in 2.4–3.8 betrays the influence of the book of Amos. The sequence of four oracles against foreign nations (2.4-15) leading up to a fifth oracle against Jerusalem (3.1-5), reflects the pattern of Amos 1.3–2.16, where (originally only four) oracles against Israel's neighbours culminate in a final oracle against the audience of Amos – Israel. The conclusion in 3.8 is patterned on Amos 4.6-12. In both cases a series of five (five occurrences of the refrain in Amos 4.6-11, five OAN in Zeph. 2.4–3.5) culminates in a command ('prepare to meet your God' in Amos 4.12, 'wait for my rising' in Zeph. 3.8) which is ambiguous and can be understood both in a positive and threatening sense (Hadjiev 2010: 329–31). All this suggests that the second iteration of the developing book of Zephaniah (1.1–3.8), like the first (1.1–2.3), was a literary enterprise which utilized prior written, and possibly some oral, traditions.

Other texts have also been seen as providing a background to Zephaniah's OAN. Berlin (1995) suggests that the conflict between Judah, on the one hand, and the Assyrian Empire and its vassals, on the other, is presented with a reference to the 'mythopoetic theme' of Genesis 10 as a conflict between the descendants of Shem (shepherds) and Ham (city dwellers). Floyd (2000: 205–13), who includes the material in chapter three into consideration, discerns a reference to the story of Babel (Gen. 11.1-9) and the mythical geography of Gen. 2.10-14.

The provenance of the OAN

In thinking about the provenance of the OAN, one has to distinguish between the origin and setting of the individual oracles and of the written composition into which they were merged. Most scholars trace at least some of the oracles back to Zephaniah, but there is no agreement on how many and which exactly come from him. Opinions vary from almost everything to almost nothing:

- Five oracles: Philistines (2.4), Philistines (2.5-7a), Moab and Ammon (2.8-9a), Cush (2.12), Assyria (2.13-15) (Ryou 1995: 296–310, 313–19).

- Three oracles: Philistines (2.4-6), Moab and Ammon (2.9a), Assyria (2.13-15) (Dietrich 2016: 232–3).
- Three oracles: Philistines (2.4), Philistines (2.5-6), Assyria (with the statement about Cush as an introduction: 2.12-14) (Irsigler 2002: 211).
- Three oracles: Philistines (2.4-7a), Cushite fragment (2.12), Assyria (2.13-14) (Edler 1984: 229-248).
- One oracle: Philistia, Moab and Ammon (2.4-5, 8-9) (Hagedorn 2011a: 113–29, 2011b).
- One oracle: Assyria (2.13-14) (Fohrer 1974: 13–22).
- Perlitt (2004: 123–31) sees no connection between 2.4-15 and the seventh century. The oracles are, in his view, too general to be tied to any specific situation from the monarchic period and the saying against Assyria is dependent on the anti-Babylonian oracle of Deutero-Isaiah (Isa. 45.6; 46.9).

Overall, the oracles against Philistia (2.4-6) and Assyria (2.13-14[15]) are generally attributed to Zephaniah. The oracle against Moab and Ammon (2.8-10) is often suspected as late because the accusation that these peoples have 'taunted' Judah and 'boasted' against its territory seem to presuppose the Babylonian exile, but many attribute at least a fragment of it (2.9a) to the prophet. The statement on the Cushites (2.12) is the most problematic of all. Some see it as an independent fragment, others as an integral part of the following Assyria oracle, still others as a later addition. It is not clear if the verbless sentence describes a past event (the defeat of the Cushite dynasty that ruled over Egypt by the Assyrians in the first half of the seventh century) or a future threat (the prospective demise of Egypt/Assyria). It is also debated whether Cush refers to (i) the Cushite kingdom to the south of Egypt, (ii) to Egypt itself or (iii) to Mesopotamia (Berlin 1994: 111–14).

As far as the provenance of the compilation as a whole is concerned, some tie it to the time of Josiah and others to the exilic period. Both positions are based on the particular choice of nations in the series, taking into account the curious fact that neither Edom nor Babylon, nor Egypt is mentioned, but work from different assumptions as to why precisely these nations were selected. Those who argue for a Josianic date assume that the threats contain genuine predictions and argue that the choice of nations fits the geopolitical situation of the seventh century (Berlin 1995; Vlaardingerboek 1999; Sweeney, 2001: 193–4; O'Brien 2004: 118, 120; Kahn 2009; Welch 2013). The series culminates with an announcement of the demise of the Assyrian Empire which fits the policy of national independence Josiah is thought to have pursued. The neighbours to the east and the west were rivals of the Judean kingdom and Assyrian vassals. Edom's absence from the OAN is easily explicable in a pre-exilic composition, since relations between Judah and Edom were amicable at that time. After the destruction of Jerusalem the Edomites became the focus of violent Judean resentment as a result of their collaboration with the Babylonians (see above on Obadiah, pp. 45–7) and their absence from 2.4-15 would be strange were this an exilic composition. Christensen (1984) proposes that Zephaniah 2.4-15 was originally aimed at supporting Josiah's policy of territorial expansion, although this proposal is problematic because the expansion policy it presumes does not match what we know about Josiah's reign from other sources.

The proponents of an exilic date assume that the threatened destruction of these nations has already taken place and this is the reason why they are included in the series. Nineveh was captured in 612 BCE, the Philistine cities were overrun by the Babylonians at the end of the seventh century and Moab and Ammon were conquered in 581 BCE. According to Seybold (1985: 88), the OAN provide the exilic Judean community with an 'aetiology of their present' reality. They present the demise of the neighbouring nations as a paradigm of Yahweh's judgement. Floyd (2000: 204) suggests that the series paints a picture of a world transformation in the context of which Judah also has to be transformed or destroyed. In the opinion of Ben Zvi (1991: 298–306) the aim of the OAN is to present Zephaniah as a reliable prophet whose earlier pronouncements have come to pass, and so to strengthen the confidence of the reader in the promises of salvation that come in the latter part of the book and still lie in the future. Edom, which was destroyed around 550 BCE, is not mentioned in Zephaniah 2, therefore the composition must be dated sometime between 580 and 550 BCE (Irsigler, 2002: 216–18).

Zephaniah 1.1–3.8 and the Babylonian exile

If 2.4-15 did not exist independently but were from the start intended to be part of a larger composition, their provenance and message must be examined not in isolation but in conjunction with this larger context. Seybold (1985: 83–93) argues that the book of Zephaniah, originally consisting of Zeph. 1.1–3.10*, was first created during the time of the exile by deuteronomistic circles. Up until that time the oracles of the prophet existed in written form independently. The deuteronomistic redactors arranged them together and added several passages, most importantly the superscription (1.1) which links Zephaniah to the Deuteronomistic History and the passage in 1.4-6 which draws on the descriptions of Josiah's reforms in 2 Kings 23. Their aim was not so much to preserve the inherited tradition as to see what was the relevance and meaning of that tradition to their own situation. The overall composition interpreted the events surrounding the destruction of Jerusalem as the arrival of the Day of the Lord announced by the prophet. It underscored Yahweh's righteousness in meting out the judgement (3.5) and pointed out that Judah's dire fate had been avoidable if only the people had heeded the prophet's words. Seybold includes 3.8-10 as the original conclusion of that script and, therefore, believes that it also contained a remarkably positive message. Beyond the judgement of the Day of the Lord there lies a purification of all nations in stark reversal of the story of the tower of Babel (Genesis 11).

The theory of an exilic deuteronomistic composition, or redaction, has been linked in recent decades to the increasingly popular book of the Twelve theory, which was discussed in chapter one (Schart 1998: 204–33; Albertz 2003a: 204–37; Wöhrle 2006: 224–6). Its proponents argue that an early version of Zephaniah's oracles (Zeph. 1.7–2.4 Albertz 2003a: 220; Zeph. 1.2-18 Wöhrle 2006: 200–1, 224) was taken up and expanded by the deuteronomistic editors and incorporated together with Hosea, Amos and Micah into a new literary work, called 'The Book of the Four (Prophets)'. The superscriptions of these four books are similar in that they all date the activities of the prophets with reference to the reigns of kings mentioned in the Deuteronomistic History. Moreover, Zephaniah, which was placed in the final position in the collection, mentions in its superscription the two great heroes of the deuteronomists – Hezekiah and Josiah – and thus establishes a connection not just with the book of Kings, but also with Hos. 1.1 and Mic. 1.1 where Hezekiah also features. Thus in its totality the book of the Four covers the history of the prophetic ministry to the two kingdoms from the time of Hezekiah in the eighth century to the reign of Josiah in the seventh. It presents the demise of the Northern kingdom (Hosea and Amos) as a paradigm for the judgement experienced by Judah, which did not heed the words of Micah and Zephaniah (Nogalski 1993a: 176). It also interpreted the Babylonian exile as a purifying judgement by means of which God intended radically to renew the life of Israel (Albertz 2003b).

This theory, however, fails to convince. The language of Zephaniah is not deuteronomistic (Ben Zvi 1999; Beck 2005: 120–2). There is some similarity between the superscriptions of the four prophetic books, but this is not enough to postulate they were part of a comprehensive redaction, because the structural, thematic and linguistic links between these books are not sufficiently strong to suggest they were ever meant to be read as part of a single whole (Hadjiev 2010: 326–32).

It is also doubtful if Zeph. 1.1–3.8 really presupposes the Babylonian exile. There is a conspicuous lack of details to tie the text specifically to the events of 587 BCE: no mention of the burning of the temple, deportation of the population or the end of the monarchy. In 3.6-7 there is talk of universal devastation (1.18; 3.8) which has already befallen the nations, but the language is generic and the assumption is that this devastation is still only a potential threat to Judah, that is, something could be done to avert it. The conclusion of the composition (3.6-7) assumes that the threats announced against the foreign nations (2.4-15) have already come to pass, but with regard to Assyria and Philistia at least this was already a reality by the end of the seventh century. The same passage interprets that devastation as a warning to Judah and chides the rebellious nation for not heeding that warning (3.2, 7). If the statements in 3.2, 7 are understood to mean that Jerusalem had its chance to heed instruction and missed it, it would be natural to conclude that Zeph. 1.1–3.8 is looking back on the events of the Babylonian conquest. However, these statements could also be taken as criticism of current behaviour. Jerusalem has been and is still refusing to trust in Yahweh (3.2). He hopes they would accept correction, but instead they corrupt their deeds (3.7).

Zephaniah 1.1–3.8 and the Judean politics in the late monarchic period

The Babylonian advance in Syria and Palestine, prior to the second capture of Jerusalem, provides a more plausible background for the text of Zeph. 1.1–3.8 (Hyatt 1948; Williams 1963; cf. Albertz 2003a: 220; Wöhrle 2006: 200–1, 224). Neef (1999: 544–5) dates the composition of Zeph. 1.1–3.8* by a disciple of the prophet to 622–612 BCE. Striek (1999: 227–33) argues that around 604 BCE Zephaniah himself composed the first edition of his book (1.3b–3.8*) on the basis of his earlier preaching, utilizing various sayings that he had pronounced during the reign of Josiah. Striek bases this dating on two main considerations. First, the calls to seek (2.3) and wait (3.8) for

Yahweh presuppose that the Day of the Lord is an impending, but still future, reality. This suggests a date prior to the fall of Jerusalem in 587 BCE, and perhaps even prior to the first capture of Jerusalem in 597 BCE. Second, the composition regards Zephaniah's earlier oracles against foreign nations (2.4-7; 2.13-14) as fulfilled (3.6), culminating with the word against Nineveh (2.13-15) which fell in 612 BCE. This suggests that the rise of the Babylonians is interpreted as a fulfilment of the prophet's earlier proclamations of the Day of the Lord. The book was composed in the aftermath of the Babylonian victory at Carchemish (605 BCE) as a warning to Judah.

A slightly later date is preferred by Irsigler (2002: 60–1, 359) and Dietrich (2016: 189–90) – the decade between the first and the second capture of Jerusalem (597–587 BCE). Dutcher-Walls (1991) has analysed the politics of that period as driven by different factions within the elite who put forward rival religious claims to support and legitimize their political programmes and thus to influence the direction of the state. The dividing lines between such power blocks lay along political ideologies and possibly family associations. In her view, a deuteronomic faction which came into existence during the time of Josiah in later years advocated submission to Babylonian power. It was opposed by a different faction which stressed the inviolability of Jerusalem. Albertz (1994: 232–41) thinks in terms of a clash between a pro-Babylonian party and a national-religious party which pushed for independence from Babylon with Egyptian support (Kratz 2015a: 54–5, 2015b: 31).

Dietrich (2016: 189–90) suggests that Zeph. 1.1–3.8 was composed to be used as part of these internal debates on the side of those who advocated submission to Babylon. If this is correct, the text's call to 'seek Yahweh' (2.3) and 'wait' for him (3.8) was originally a call to pursue a specific international policy. The princes, judges, prophets and priests (3.4) targeted by the scroll were not the whole Judean aristocracy but the faction in Jerusalem which advocated alliance with Egypt and rebellion against Babylon. The authors of this edition of Zephaniah believed that such a policy betrays a lack of trust in Yahweh and feared it would lead to Judah being engulfed in the destruction of the nations which Yahweh was bringing through the Babylonians.

Further study

On the background of the OAN in Zephaniah see the studies of Christensen 1984; Berlin 1995; Ryou 1995; Sweeney 2001; Kahn 2009; Welch 2013.

Of the commentaries useful discussions can be found in Floyd 2000 and Irsigler 2002.

For a pre-exilic dating of 1.1–3.8 see Striek 1999 and consult also Neef 1999; Irsigler 2002; Dietrich 2016. On the factions in Judean politics in the late monarchic period see Dutcher-Walls 1991 and Albertz 1994.

An exilic deuteronomistic redaction of Zephaniah is argued by Seybold 1985 and is connected to the 'book of the Four' hypothesis by Nogalski 1993a; Schart 1998; Albertz 2003a, 2003b; Wöhrle 2006. For criticism see Ben Zvi 1999; Hadjiev 2010; Levin 2011b.

17

Zephaniah's message of hope (3.9-20) and the canonical shape of the book

Chapter Outline

The salvation of the remnant (2.3*, 7, 9b; 3.11-13)	115
The turning of the nations (2.11; 3.9-10)	117
The joy of Zion (3.14-20)	119
Reading Zephaniah as Scripture	120
Further study	121

The end of the book of Zephaniah looks to the future and promises restoration. These promises deal with different groups of people: (i) the nations (3.9-10), (ii) the remnant (3.11-13) and (iii) Zion (3.14-20). Two of those themes have already appeared in the preceding material. The turning of the nations to Yahweh is anticipated in 2.11 and the salvation of the remnant, in 2.7, 9.

The salvation of the remnant (2.3*, 7, 9b; 3.11-13)

The theme of the remnant appears for the first time in Zeph. 2.3. While the opening call is addressed to the whole 'shameless' or 'worthless' nation (2.1) in 2.3 it is only 'the humble of the earth who do his justice' that are called to seek Yahweh. The reader is left unsure whether the 'nation' of 2.1 and 'all the humble' of 2.3 are the same or not. It is also not clear why the humble who are already doing Yahweh's justice are threatened with punishment and called to seek humility and justice in order to avoid it. Probably the phrase 'all the humble of the land who do his justice' is an addition to 2.3 which redirects the text to a different group of addressees.

This same group reappears at the end of the oracles against the Philistines, and Moab and Ammon. There it is called 'the remnant of the house of Judah' (2.7) and 'the rest of my nation' (2.9b) and it is promised to inherit the devastated and depopulated lands of these nations. As a result of the divine judgement the coastal plain will become shepherds' pastures and folds for flocks (2.6) upon which the remnant will graze (2.7). There is an interesting link with the Assyria oracle, which does not mention the remnant directly, but also envisages flocks grazing in the midst of the ruins of Nineveh and Ashur (2.14). The reader is left to wonder whether the metaphorical Judean flock is not promised here an even bigger grazing field once the judgement dust has settled. The last passage to deal with that theme is 3.11-13. It sees the punishment of Jerusalem as aimed at purification, because it removes from the holy mountain all arrogant and deceitful people, whose deeds have brought only shame. The 'remnant of Israel', people 'humble and poor', seeking refuge in the name of Yahweh will remain there to 'feed and graze', as they did in chapter two, without fear.

The designation of the remnant as 'poor and humble' can be taken in two different ways: as a literal description of their economic status, or as a metaphorical depiction of their spirituality. The language of poverty and oppression appears in the Psalms to describe metaphorically the worshippers of Yahweh and their enemies. Ben Zvi (1991: 147–50, 234–8, 322–3) highlights the links of such descriptions with Zephaniah and argues for a metaphorical interpretation. Likewise, Ro (2002: 83–112) holds that the poverty in Zephaniah has nothing to do with material poverty. It depicts a religious attitude of people who rely on God's help and expect to experience deliverance in the eschatological future. It serves to convey a relationship of total dependence on God and at the same time to distinguish the community of the redactor from other, hostile groups.

Weigl (1994: 99–121), on the other hand, accepts a literal interpretation. According to him in chapter one Zephaniah announces judgement on the elite, living in the city and in 2.1-3 he addresses the poor people of the countryside who 'have no silver' and, like the oppressed Israelites in Egypt (Exod. 5.7), 'gather straw'. These poor people have the opportunity to seek Yahweh, to be delivered on the day of judgement and consequently to become the 'remnant of Israel' in Jerusalem (3.12-13). The book does not equate poverty with righteousness, but economic status, righteous behaviour and religious attitude are closely linked. In Zephaniah the rich appear as wicked and the poor – as righteous (Weigl 1994: 215–16). Gorgulho (1991) also identifies the poor with the Judean farmers who were exploited under the Assyrian imperialistic system but interprets Zephaniah's call to seek righteousness (2.3) as a call to achieve liberation for the oppressed. The aim of this liberation project is the creation of a community without social stratification (3.11-13) where Yahweh reigns (3.14-15). Thus the book of Zephaniah provides hope for the poor of all generations.

As pointed out earlier, the phrase 'all the humble of the land who do his justice' in 2.3 is a later addition to the text. The same is true of the remnant passages in the OAN (2.7 and 2.9a) and of 3.11-13 which was composed as a new conclusion to bring the idea of the remnant central to these additions to the fore (Hadjiev 2011: 576–8). It is best, therefore, with Albertz (2003a: 223–4) and Wöhrle (2008b), to see the 'humble and poor' of Zephaniah as the remnant that survived the Babylonian deportations and remained in Palestine. Its presence in the text underlines a positive aspect of the judgement: it purifies the nation and gives an opportunity for a new start, a utopian future (3.11-13) free from the corruption of the past.

The turning of the nations (2.11; 3.9-10)

Two passages widen the horizon beyond the borders of Israel to include in the future era of restoration the nations as well. Right at the centre of the OAN, between the oracles against the Philistines (2.4-7) and Moab and Ammon (2.8-10), on the one hand, and the oracles against Cush (2.12) and Assyria (2.13-15), on the other, there is a brief statement which promises a terrifying divine action against 'all the gods of the earth' followed by worship offered to Yahweh by 'every man in his place' and all the 'islands of the nations' (2.11). The second passage opens up the series of oracles of restoration (3.9-10). In it God promises to give to the peoples 'pure language' so that they can call on his name and serve him in unity, bringing gifts even from beyond the rivers of Cush. This passage is a textbook example of intertextuality. The first part reverses the tower of Babel story in which disunity of the nations is linked to their diverse languages (Genesis 11). The second part not only draws on the language and ideas of Isaiah 18.1, 7 but also reflects more generally the OT idea of the nations worshipping in Jerusalem in the eschatological future.

Syntactically and thematically these verses sit uneasily in their literary context, suggesting they are later additions to the book, which reinterpret Zephaniah's vision of the future by giving it a more universalistic outlook (Hadjiev 2011: 574–5). Petersen (2011) argues that the idea of the 'nations' as a generic concept, who worship Yahweh, is a new element in the prophetic tradition which entered during the Second Temple period under the influence of the Psalms.

The main interpretative question is how these different ideas fit together at the level of the final form of the text. Oeming (1987) suggests that two contradictory ideas stand behind the text of Zeph. 3.1-13. In the original prophetic proclamation the nations were used as a tool in the judgement of Jerusalem in 3.8 and immediately following that (3.9-10), together with the righteous remnant, converted to Yahweh. A later nationalistic hand altered the original 'you' in 3.8 to 'them', converting the threat of the outpouring of the divine anger against Judah into a proclamation of the punishment of the nations.

Weigl (1994: 132–4) attempts to integrate the various pictures within Zephaniah into one coherent scenario without recourse to diachronic solutions. According to him in chapter two we encounter two groups of people that stand in parallel to one another – the 'humble of the land' from 2.1-3 and the 'islands of the nations' in 2.11. They are similar because they both stand at the periphery away from the centres of power, form a positive relationship with Yahweh through worship, and survive the impending catastrophe. In 3.9-13 both groups meet in Jerusalem to merge together and form the core of a renewed community. Timmer (2015b) offers a similar reading according to which 3.9 describes a remnant of the nations, parallel to the faithful remnant of Judah. These verses place Israel and the nations on equal footing (Lo 2011: 146–7).

This is a possible, although not a necessary, way of reading the final form of the text because the language of 2.11 and 3.9-10 implies that different groups of people may be in view. The promise of 3.9 identifies the travellers to Jerusalem neither as the 'remnant' nor as the 'islands' of the nations. Since in 2.11 Yahweh acts against 'all the gods of the earth' and the result is that 'every man in his place' worships him, it is possible that the 'islands of the nations' are just a way of saying that everybody, even to the ends of the earth, will worship Yahweh. This, then, would be the climax, not a preliminary step, in the process of the conversion of the world. In this scenario Jerusalem does not play a universal role. The redactors may not have intended these pictures to be read in a linear fashion but rather as partial, unrelated glimpses into a glorious future.

Beck (2008) argues that chapter three presents a composite picture of the Day of Yahweh which was built by the addition of different redactional passages. In 3.1-8 the Day of Yahweh is an apocalyptic event of universal judgement when God pours out his wrath on all the earth. This is qualified in 3.14-15 where Yahweh shows himself also to be a God of grace who reverses judgement on his people and annihilates their enemies. The additions in 3.11-13 and 3.9-10 introduce a different picture, the salvation of a humble remnant from Judah and from the nations after the apocalyptic judgement unfolds. It is possible that these pictures offer different visions of salvation that result from a dialogue within the post-exilic community (Hadjiev 2011) and were never intended to portray a coherent story.

The joy of Zion (3.14-20)

Sweeney (2003a: 194) sees the promises expressed in this passage as an important part of the prophet's rhetorical strategy. Because the end of the Assyrian oppression is neigh and Jerusalem is about to take up again its place as Yahweh's holy abode on earth, the audience is urged to heed the call to seek Yahweh and join King Josiah in his drive to reform the cult. Salvation then is subordinated to the overarching exhortation and serves as its motivation. More often, however, interpreters see 3.14-20 as the main point of the book in its final form. According to the often adopted tripartite structure of Zephaniah, the concluding passage of hope is the climax towards which the prophecy inexorably is moving. Sin and judgement are real, but they do not have the final say.

Most critics also regard these verses as later additions. The promise of the ingathering of the exiles and reversal of the shameful state of weakness and oppression seems to presuppose the events of the Babylonian deportations, and so a time period later than the purported date of Zephaniah's ministry. More importantly, it is difficult to see how the unconditional message of restoration and deliverance in this passage can derive from the same historical situation as the vehement criticisms of chapter one and the accompanying proclamation of unavoidable judgement. It is true that a message of judgement and salvation are not theologically or psychologically incompatible. Theologically they express different sides of God's character and his relation to humanity. To suggest that a prophet could only preach judgement or mercy but never both is ridiculous.

The point, however, is that these two types of message are *rhetorically* incompatible. In other words they cannot be proclaimed simultaneously within the same context because then they will cancel each other. Either the message of judgement will overshadow hope, or the announcement of salvation will relativize the judgement. For a preacher of judgement to feel the need to announce hope a new rhetorical situation must come into existence. Therefore, 3.14-20 are best regarded as a series of exilic, or post-exilic, additions to the book of Zephaniah that sought to update its message and make it relevant to a new historical situation.

Reading Zephaniah as Scripture

This raises the question how is one to read best the text of Zephaniah that we now possess. Many readers assume that because the final canonical form of the text has come to us through tradition we need to focus exclusively on it. This, however, is neither feasible in practice nor methodologically advisable. Every reader approaches the text with a lens which causes them to ignore some aspects of the text and focus on other. Readers construe the relationships of the textual features differently and fill textual gaps in a varying ways. An important factor in this process is the situation and the interests of the reader.

A reading of the final form of the book of Zephaniah that sees its goal and major theme in the concluding sections with their focus on the deliverance and the reversal of fortunes would be particularly appropriate to people whose situation resembles somehow the circumstances of the exilic and post-exilic communities where the text originally crystallized. The prophecy can offer a message of hope to those who are poor, oppressed, marginalized and persecuted.

The text will have to speak differently to people who enjoy power and wealth. There is enough material in the earlier parts of Zephaniah to challenge those who are at the top. The prophecy could be read as a call to such people to emend their ways and as a dire warning of the ultimate consequences of idolatry and injustice. Such a reading will necessarily have to ignore or downplay the final hopeful sections of the book which will be irrelevant for such a task. It will have to stop at 2.3 or 3.8 and read Zephaniah in its earlier pre-exilic stages of redaction when it was addressed to the Judean aristocracy. The centre of attention will have to shift from the epilogue of the book (3.14-20) to the middle (2.1-3) and treat (once again!) the prophecy not as a promise but as an exhortation. In making such a hermeneutical move it is beneficial to recognize that the redaction history of the book serves as its basis and justification.

Further study

On the identification of the remnant and its description as poor and humble compare the different perspectives found in Sweeney 2003a; Gafney 2017; with Ben Zvi 1991; Ro 2002; with Weigl 1994; Gorgulho 1991; and with Albertz 2003a; Wöhrle 2008b. More broadly on the remnant see Lo 2011. The turning of the nations to Yahweh is discussed by Oeming 1987; Weigl 1994; Timmer 2015b. On chapter three as a redactional collage of different pictures of salvation see Beck 2008; Hadjiev 2011.

Bibliography

Adu-Gyamfi, Y. (2015), 'God's Wrath and Judgement on Ethnic Hatred and Hope for Victims of Ethnic Hatred in Obadiah: Implications for Africa', *OTE* 28: 11–30.

Ahlström, G. W. (1971), *Joel and the Temple Cult of Jerusalem*, VTSup 21; Leiden: Brill.

Albertz, R. (1994), *A History of Israelite Religion in the Old Testament Period*, trans. J. Bowden, OTL; Louisville: Westminster/John Knox Press.

Albertz, R. (2003a), *Israel in Exile: The History and Literature of the Sixth Century BCE*, trans. D. Green, Studies in Biblical Literature; Atlanta: SBL.

Albertz, R. (2003b), 'Exile as Purification. Reconstructing the "Book of the Four"', in P. L. Redditt and A. Schart (eds), *Thematic Threads in the Book of the Twelve*, 232–51, BZAW 325; Berlin and New York: W. de Gruyter.

Albertz, R. (2007), 'Why a Reform Like Josiah's Must Have Happened', in L. L. Grabbe (ed.), *Good Kings and Bad Kings: The Kingdom of Judah in the Seventh Century BCE*, 27–46, London and New York: T&T Clark.

Allen, L. C. (1976), *The Books of Joel, Obadiah, Jonah and Micah*, NICOT; Grand Rapids: Eerdmans.

Andersen, F. I. (2001), *Habakkuk: A New Translation with Introduction and Commentary*, AB 25; New York: Doubleday.

Anderson, B. A. (2010), 'Poetic Justice in Obadiah', *JSOT* 35: 247–55.

Anderson, B. A. (2011), *Brotherhood and Inheritance: A Canonical Reading of the Esau and Edom Traditions*, LHBOTS 556; New York and London: Bloomsbury T&T Clark.

Anderson, B. A. (2013–2014), 'The Reception of Obadiah: Some Historical, Ideological, and Visual Considerations', *Proceedings of the Irish Biblical Association* 36–37: 17–35.

Anderson, J. E. (2011), 'Awaiting an Answered Prayer: The Development and Reinterpretation of Habakkuk 3 in its Contexts', *ZAW* 122: 57–71.

Andiñach, P.R. (1992), 'The Locusts in the Message of Joel', *VT* 42: 433–41.

Assis, E. (2006), 'Why Edom? On the Hostility Towards Jacob's Brother in Prophetic Sources', *VT* 56: 1–20.

Assis, E. (2013), *The Book of Joel: A Prophet between Calamity and Hope*, LHBOTS 581; New York: Bloomsbury.

Assis, E. (2014), 'Structure, Redaction and Significance in the Prophecy of Obadiah', *JSOT* 39: 209–21.

Assis, E. (2016), *Identity in Conflict: The Struggle Between Esau and Jacob, Edom and Israel*, Siphrut 19; Winona Lake: Eisenbrauns.

Bail, U. (2012), 'Habakkuk: A Political Night-Prayer', in L. Schottroff and M.-T. Wacker (eds), *Feminist Biblical Interpretation: A Companion of Critical Commentary on the Books of the Bible and Related Literature*, 443–9, Grand Rapids and Cambridge: Eerdmans.

Barker, J. (2014), *From the Depths of Despair to the Promise of Presence: A Rhetorical Reading of the Book of Joel*, Siphrut 11; Winona Lake: Eisenbrauns.

Barker, K. L. and Bailey, W. (1998), *Micah, Nahum, Habakkuk, Zephaniah*, NAC 20; Nashville: B&H.

Barre, M. L. (2013), 'Newly Discovered Literary Devices in the Prayer of Habakkuk', *CBQ* 75: 446–62.

Bartlett, J. R. (1989), *Edom and the Edomites*, JSOTSup 77; Sheffield: JSOT Press.

Barton, J. (2001), *Joel and Obadiah: A Commentary*, OTL; Louisville: Westminster John Knox Press.

Barton, J. (2004), 'The Day of Yahweh in the Minor Prophets', in C. McCarthy and J. F. Healey (eds), *Biblical and Near Eastern Essays: FS K.J. Cathcart*, 68–79, JSOTSup 375; London and New York: T&T Clark.

Barton, J. (2014), *Ethics in Ancient Israel*, Oxford: Oxford University Press.

Beck, M. (2005), *Der 'Tag YHWHs im Dodekapropheton: Studien im Spannungsfeld von Traditions- und Redaktionsgeschichte'*, BZAW 356; Berlin and New York: W. de Gruyter.

Beck, M. (2006), 'Das Dodekapropheton als Anthologie', *ZAW* 118: 558–81.

Beck, M. (2008), 'Das Tag-YHWHs-Verständnis von Zephanja iii', *VT* 58: 159–77.

Beit-Arieh, I. (1989), 'New Data on the Relationship Between Judah and Edom Towards the End of the Iron Age', in S. Gitin and E. G. Dever (eds), *Recent Excavations in Israel: Studies in Iron Age Archaeology*, 125–31, Annual of the American Schools of Oriental Research 49; Winona Lake: Eisenbrauns.

Bellinger Jr., W. H. (1984), *Psalmody and Prophecy*, JSOTSup 27; Sheffield: JSOT Press.

Ben Zvi, E. (1991), *A Historical-Critical Study of the Book of Zephaniah*, BZAW 198; Berlin and New York: W. de Gruyter.

Ben Zvi, E. (1996a), *A Historical-Critical Study of the Book of Obadiah*, BZAW 242; Berlin and New York: W. de Gruyter.

Ben Zvi, E. (1996b), 'Studying Prophetic Texts Against Their Original Backgrounds: Pre-Ordained Scripts and Alternative Horizons of Research', in S. B. Reid (ed.), *Prophets and Paradigms: FS G.M. Tucker*, 125–35, JSOTSup 229; Sheffield: Sheffield Academic Press.

Ben Zvi, E. (1996c), 'Twelve Prophetic Books or "The Twelve"? A Few Preliminary Considerations', in J. W. Watts and P. R. House (eds), *Forming Prophetic Literature. FS J. D.W. Watts*, 125–56, JSOTSup 235; Sheffield: Sheffield Academic Press.

Ben Zvi, E. (1999), 'A Deuteronomistic Redaction in/among "The Twelve"? A Contribution from the Standpoint of the Books of Micah, Zephaniah and Obadiah', in L. S. Schearing and S. L. McKenzie (eds), *Those Elusive Deuteronomists: The Phenomenon of Pan-Deuteronomism*, 232–61, JSOTSup 268; Sheffield: Sheffield Academic Press.

Ben Zvi, E. (2007), 'Josiah and the Prophetic Books: Some Observations', in L. L. Grabbe (ed.), *Good Kings and Bad Kings: The Kingdom of Judah in the Seventh Century BCE*, 47–64, London and New York: T&T Clark.

Ben Zvi, E. (2009a), 'The Concept of Prophetic Books and Its Historical Setting', in D. V. Edelman and E. Ben Zvi (eds), *The Production of Prophecy: Constructing Prophecy and Prophets in Yehud*, 73–95, London and Oakville: Equinox.

Ben Zvi, E. (2009b), 'Is the Twelve Hypothesis Likely from an Ancient Readers' Perspective?' in E. Ben Zvi and J. D. Nogalski (eds), *Two Sides of a Coin: Juxtaposing Views on Interpreting the Book of the Twelve/the Twelve Prophetic Books*, 47–96, Analecta Gorgiana 201; Piscataway: Gorgias Press.

Bergler, S. (1988), *Joel als Schriftinterpret*, Beiträge zur Erforschung des Alten Testaments und des Antiken Judentums 16; Frankfurt am Main: Peter Lang.

Berlin, A. (1994), *Zephaniah: A New Translation with Introduction and Commentary*, AB 25A; New York and London: Doubleday.

Berlin, A. (1995), 'Zephaniah's Oracle Against the Nations and an Israelite Cultural Myth', in A. B. Beck, A. H. Bartelt, P. R. Raabe and C. A. Franke (eds), *Fortunate the Eyes That See: FS D.N. Freedman*, 175–84, Grand Rapids and Cambridge: Eerdmans.

Bernat, D. A. and Klawans, J. (eds) (2007), *Religion and Violence: The Biblical Heritage*, Recent Research in Biblical Studies 2; Sheffield: Sheffield Phoenix Press.

Bewer, J. A. (1911), *Obadiah and Joel*, ICC; Edinburgh: T&T Clark.

Blenkinsopp, J. (1996), *A History of Prophecy in Israel: Revised and Enlarged*, 2nd edn, Louisville and London: Westminster John Knox Press.

Blenkinsopp, J. (2008), 'The Midianite-Kenite Hypothesis Revisited and the Origins of Judah', *JSOT* 33: 131–53.

Block, D. I. (2017), *Obadiah: The Kingship Belongs to YHWH*, Zondervan Exegetical Commentary on the Old Testament; Grand Rapids: Zondervan.

Boadt, L. (1982), *Jeremiah 26-52, Habakkuk, Zephaniah, Nahum*, Wilmington: Michael Glazier.

Bosshard-Nepustil, E. (1997), *Rezeptionen von Jesaia 1-39 im Zwölfprophetenbuch: Untersuchungen zur literarischen Verbindung von*

Prophetenbüchern in babylonischer und persischer Zeit, Orbis Biblicus
  Et Orientalis 154; Freiburg, Schweiz and Göttingen: Universitätsverlag /
  Vandenhoeck & Ruprecht.
Bruckner, J. (2004), *Jonah, Nahum, Habakkuk, Zephaniah*, NIV Application
  Commentary; Grand Rapids: Zondervan.
Carvalho, C. (2010), 'The Beauty of the Bloody God: The Divine Warrior in
  Prophetic Literature', in J. M. O'Brien and C. Franke (eds), *The Aesthetics
  of Violence in the Prophets*, 131–52, LHBOTS 517; New York and London:
  T&T Clark.
Cathcart, K. J. (2010), '"Law is Paralysed" (Habakkuk 1.4): Habakkuk's
  Dialogue with God and the Language of Legal Disputation', in J. Day (ed.),
  Prophecy and the Prophets in Ancient Israel, 339–53, LHBOTS 531; London
  and New York: T&T Clark.
Chitsulo, T. S. (2015), 'Exploring the Role of the Wicked in Habakkuk from
  Malawi Socio-Economic and Political Viewpoint', *OTE* 28: 301–25.
Christensen, D. L. (1975), *Prophecy and War in Ancient Israel: Studies in the
  Oracles Against the Nations in Old Testament Prophecy*, Berkley: Bibal Press.
Christensen, D. L. (1984), 'Zephaniah 2:4-15: A Theological Basis for Josiah's
  Program of Political Expansion', *CBQ* 46: 669–82.
Claassens, L. J. (2012), *Mourner, Mother, Midwife: Reimagining God's Delivering
  Presence in the Old Testament*, Louisville: Westminster John Knox Press.
Claassens, L. J. (2016), 'God and Violence in the Prophets', in C. J. Sharp (ed.),
  The Oxford Handbook of the Prophets, 334–49, Oxford: Oxford University
  Press.
Cleaver-Bartholomew, D. (2004), 'An Alternative Reading of Hab 1 and 2',
  Proceedings 24: 45–59.
Cogan, M. (1974), *Imperialism and Religion: Assyria, Judah and Israel in the
  Eighth and Ceventh Centuries BCE*, SBLMS 19; Missoula: Scholars Press.
Coggins, R. J. (1982), 'An Alternative Prophetic Tradition', in R. Coggins, M.
  A. Knibb and A. Phillips (eds), *Israel's Prophetic Tradition: FS Peter Ackroyd*,
  77–94, Cambridge: Cambridge University Press.
Coggins, R. J. (1985), *Israel among the Nations: A Commentary on the Books of
  Nahum and Obadiah*, ITC; Grand Rapids and Edinburgh: Eerdmans and
  Handsel.
Coggins, R. J. (2000), *Joel and Amos*, New Century Bible Commentary;
  Sheffield: Sheffield Academic Press.
Collins, J. J. (1979), 'Towards the Morphology of a Genre: Introduction', *Semeia*
  14: 1–20.
Collins, J. J. (2014), 'What is Apocalyptic Literature?' in J. J. Collins (ed.), *The
  Oxford Handbook of Apocalyptic Literature*, 1–16, Oxford: Oxford University
  Press.

Collins, J. J. (2015), *Apocalypse, Prophecy, and Pseudepigraphy: On Jewish Apocalyptic Literature*, Grand Rapids and Cambridge: Eerdmans.

Cook, S. L. (1995), *Prophecy and Apocalypticism: The Postexilic Social Setting*, Minneapolis: Portress.

Cook, S. L. (2014), 'Apocalyptic Prophecy', in J. J. Collins (ed.), *The Oxford Handbook of Apocalyptic Literature*, 18–35, Oxford: Oxford University Press.

Crenshaw, J. L. (1995), *Joel*, AB 24C; New Haven and London: Yale University Press.

Crenshaw, J. L. (2005), *Defending God: Biblical Responses to the Problem of Evil*, Oxford: Oxford University Press.

Crouch, C. L. (2011), 'Ezekiel's Oracles Against the Nations in the Light of Royal Ideology of Warfare', *JBL* 130: 473–92.

Crowell, B. L. (2007), 'Nabonidus, as-Sila', and the Beginning of the End of Edom', *Bulletin of the American Schools of Oriental Research* 348: 75–88.

Culley, R. C. (2000), 'Orality and Writtenness in Prophetic Texts', in E. Ben Zvi and M. H. Floyd (eds), *Writings and Speech in Israelite and Ancient Near Easter Prophecy*, 45–64, SBLSS 10; Atlanta: SBL.

Dahmen, U. (2001), 'Das Buch Joel', in U. Dahmen and G. Fleischer (eds), *Die Bücher Joel und Amos*, NSKAT 23.2; Stuttgart: Verlag Katholisches Bibelwerk.

Dangl, O. (2001), 'Habakkuk in Recent Research', *CR: BS* 9: 131–68.

Dangl, O. (2014), *Das Buch Habakuk*, NSKAT 25.1; Stuttgart: Verlag Katholisches Bibelwerk.

Davies, P. R. (1989), 'The Social World of Apocalyptic Writings', in R. E. Clements (ed.), *The World of Ancient Israel: Sociological, Anthropological and Political Perspectives*, 251–71, Cambridge: Cambridge University Press.

Day, J. (1985), *God's Conflict with the Dragon and the Sea: Echoes of a Canaanite Myth in the Old Testament*, Cambridge: Cambridge University Press.

Deist, F. E. (1988), 'Parallels and Reinterpretation in the Book of Joel: A Theology of the Yom Yahweh?' in W. Claassen (ed.), *Text and Context: FS F.C. Fensham*, 63–79, JSOTSup 48; Sheffield: JSOT Press.

De Jong, M. J. (2007), *Isaiah among the Ancient Near Eastern Prophets: A Comparative Study of the Earliest Stages of the Isaiah Tradition and the Neo-Assyrian Prophecies*, VTSup 117; Leiden and Boston: Brill.

Dempsey, C. J. (2000), *The Prophets: A Liberation-Critical Reading*, Minneapolis: Fortress Press.

Dicou, B. (1994), *Edom, Israel's Brother and Antagonist: The Role of Edom in Biblical Prophecy and Story*. JSOTSup 169; Sheffield: JSOT Press.

Dietrich, W. (2016), *Nahum, Habakkuk, Zephaniah*, trans. P. Altmann, International Exegetical Commentary on the Old Testament; Stuttgart: W. Kohlhammer.

Dutcher-Walls, P. (1991), 'The Social Location of the Deuteronomists: A Sociological Study of Factional Politics in Late Pre-Exilic Judah', *JSOT* 52: 77–94.

Eaton, J. (1981), *Vision in Worship: The Relation of Prophecy and Liturgy in the Old Testament*, London: SPCK.

Edler, R. (1984), *Das Kerygma des Propheten Zefanja*, Freiburger Theologische Studien 126; Freiburg, Basel and Wien: Herder.

Emerton, J. A. (1977), 'Textual and Linguistic Problems of Habakkuk 2.4-5', *JTS* 28: 1–18.

Emerton, J. A. (1982), 'New Light on Israelite Religion: The Implications of the Inscriptions from Kuntillet ʿAjrud', *ZAW* 94: 2–20.

Esler, P. F. (2014), 'Social-Scientific Approaches to Apocalyptic Literature', in J. J. Collins (ed.), *The Oxford Handbook of Apocalyptic Literature*, 123–44, Oxford: Oxford University Press.

Everson, J. A. (1974), 'The Days of Yahweh', *JBL* 93: 329–37.

Everson, J. A. (2003), 'The Canonical Location of Habakkuk', in P. L Redditt and A. Schart (eds), *Thematic Threads in the Book of the Twelve*, 165–74, BZAW 325; Berlin and New York: W. de Gruyter.

Ferreiro, A. (2003), *The Twelve Prophets*, Ancient Christian Commentary on Scripture 14; Downers Grove: IVP.

Floyd, M. H. (1991), 'Prophetic Complaints about the Fulfilment of Oracles in Habakkuk 1:2-17 and Jeremiah 15:10-18', *JBL* 110: 397–418.

Floyd, M. H. (1993), 'Prophecy and Writing in Habakkuk 2, 1-5', *ZAW* 105: 462–81.

Floyd, M. H. (2000), *Minor Prophets: Part 2*, Forms of Old Testament Literature XXII; Grand Rapids and Cambridge: Eerdmans.

Floyd, M. H. (2002), 'The מַשָּׂא (maśśāʾ) as a Type of Prophetic Book', *JBL* 121: 401–22.

Floyd, M. H. (2006), 'The Production of Prophetic Books in the Early Second Temple Period', in M. H. Floyd and R. D. Haak (eds), *Prophets, Prophecy, and Prophetic Texts in Second Temple Judaism*, 276–97, New York and London: T&T Clark.

Fohrer, G. (1974), *Die Propheten des Alten Testaments. 2. Die Propheten des 7. Jahrhunderts*, Gütersloh: Gütersloher Verlagshaus.

Fretheim, T. E. (2004), 'God and Violence in the Old Testament', *Word and World* 24: 18–28.

Fuller, R. (1996), 'The Form and Formation of the Book of the Twelve: The Evidence from the Judean Desert', in J. W. Watts and P. R. House (eds), *Forming Prophetic Literature*: FS J. D.W. Watts, 86–101, JSOTSup 235; Sheffield: Sheffield Academic Press.

Fuller, R. (1999), 'The Text of the Twelve Minor Prophets', *CR:BS* 7: 81–95.

Gafney, W. C. M. (2017), *Nahum, Habakkuk, Zephaniah*, Wisdom Commentary 38; Collegeville: Liturgical Press.

Garrett, D. A. (1997), *Hosea, Joel*, New American Commentary 19A; Nashville: B&H.

Geller, S. A. (2007), 'The Prophetic Roots of Religious Violence in Western Religions', in D. A. Bernat and J. Klawans (eds), *Religion and Violence: The Biblical Heritage*, 47–56, Recent Research in Biblical Studies 2; Sheffield: Sheffield Phoenix Press.

Geyer, J. B. (2004), *Mythology and Lament: Studies in the Oracles about the Nations*, SOTS Monographs; Hants and Burlington: Ashgate.

Geyer, J. B. (2009), 'Another Look at the Oracles about the Nations in the Hebrew Bible. A Response to A. C. Hagedorn', *VT* 59: 80–7.

Gorgulho, G. (1991), 'Zefania und die historische Bedeutung der Armen', *Evangelische Theologie* 51: 81–92.

Grabbe, L. L. (2007), *Good Kings and Bad Kings: The Kingdom of Judah in the Seventh Century BCE*, London and New York: T&T Clark.

Grund, A. (2013), 'Kritik, Unheil, erste Sammlungen. Zum altorientalischen Hintergrund der israelitischen Schriftprophetie', *BZ* 57: 216–43.

Haak, R. D. (1992), *Habakkuk*, VTSup 44; Leiden: Brill.

Haak, R. D. (2010), 'Mapping Violence in the Prophets: Zephaniah 2', in J. M. O'Brien and C. Franke (eds), *The Aesthetics of Violence in the Prophets*, 18–36, LHBOTS 517; New York and London: T&T Clark.

Hadjiev, T. S. (2009), *The Composition and Redaction of the Book of Amos*, BZAW 393; Berlin and New York: W. de Gruyter.

Hadjiev, T. S. (2010), 'Zephaniah and the "Book of the Twelve" Hypothesis', in J. Day (ed.), *Prophecy and the Prophets in Ancient Israel*, 325–38, LHBOTS 531; London and New York: T&T Clark.

Hadjiev, T. S. (2011), 'Survival, Conversion and Restoration: Reflections on the Redaction History of the Book of Zephaniah', *VT* 61: 570–81.

Hadjiev, T. S. (2012), 'The Translation Problems of Zephaniah 3,18: A Diachronic Solution', *ZAW* 124: 416–20.

Hadjiev, T. S. (2014), 'The Theological Transformations of Zephaniah's Proclamation of Doom', *ZAW* 126: 506–20.

Hadjiev, T. S. (2020), 'A Prophetic Anthology Rather than a Book of the Twelve: The Unity of the Minor Prophets Reconsidered', in L.-S. Tiemeyer and J. Wöhrle (eds), *The Book of the Twelve: Composition, Reception, and Interpretation*, Formation and Interpretation of Old Testament Literature/VTSup; Leiden: Brill.

Hagedorn, A. C. (2007), 'Looking at Foreigners in Biblical and Greek Prophecy', *VT* 57: 432–48.

Hagedorn, A. C. (2011a), *Die Anderen im Spiegel: Israels Auseinandersetzung mit den Völkern in den Büchern Nahum, Zefanja, Obadja und Joel*, BZAW 414; Berlin: W. De Gruyter.

Hagedorn, A. C. (2011b), 'When Did Zephaniah Become a Supporter of Josiah's Reform', *JTS* 62: 453–75.

Hagedorn, A. C. (2015), 'Die Perser im Zwölfprophetenbuch', *ZAW* 127: 587–606.

Heard, C. (1997), 'Hearing the Children's Cries: Commentary, Deconstruction, Ethics, and the Book of Habakkuk', *Semeia* 77: 75–89.

Herrmann, W. (2001), 'Das unerledigte Problem des Buches Habakkuk', *VT* 51: 481–96.

Hiebert, T. (1986), *God of My Victory: The Ancient Hymn in Habakkuk 3*, Harvard Semitic Monographs 38; Atlanta: Scholars Press.

Hoffmann, Y. (1981), 'The Day of the Lord as a Concept and a Term in the Prophetic Literature', *ZAW* 93: 37–50.

Holland, S. (2002), 'The Gospel of Peace and the Violence of God', *Cross Currents* 51: 470–83.

House, P. R. (1989), *Zephaniah: A Prophetic Drama*, Sheffield: Almond Press.

Hubbard, D. A. (1989), *Joel and Amos*, Tyndale Old Testament Commentary; Leicester: Inter-Varsity.

Hunn, D. (2009), 'Habakkuk 2.4b in Its Context: How Far Off Was Paul?' *JSOT* 34: 219–39.

Hurowitz, V. A. (1993), 'Joel Locust's Plague in the Light of Sargon II's Hymn to Nanaya', *JBL* 112: 597–603.

Hyatt, J. P. (1948), 'The Date and Background of Zephaniah', *Journal of Near Eastern Studies* 7: 25–9.

Irsigler, H. (2002), *Zefanja*, Herders Theologischer Kommentar zum Alten Testament; Freiburg: Herder.

Jenson, P. P. (2008), *Obadiah, Jonah, Micah: A Theological Commentary*, LHBOTS, 496; New York and London: T&T Clark.

Jeremias, J. (1970), *Kultprophetie und Gerichtsverkündigung in der späten Königszeit Israels*, WMANT 35; Neukirchen: Neukirchener Verlag.

Jeremias, J. (2000), 'Der "Tag Jahwes" in Jes 13 und Joel 2', in R. G. Kratz, T. Krüger and K. Schmid (eds), *Schriftauslegung in der Schrift: FS O.H. Steck*, 129–38, BZAW 300; Berlin and New York: W. de Gruyter.

Jeremias, J. (2007), *Die Propheten Joel, Obadja, Jona, Micha*, ATD 24.3; Göttingen: Vandenhoeck & Ruprecht.

Jeremias, J. (2012), 'The Function of the Book of Joel for Reading the Twelve', in R. Alberts, J. Nogalski and J. Wöhrle (eds), *Perspectives on the Formation of the Book of the Twelve: Methodological Foundations — Redactional Processes — Historical Insights*, 77–87, BZAW 433; Berlin and New York: W. de Gruyter.

Jeremias, J. (2017), 'Three Theses on the Early History of Israel', in J. van Oorschot and M. Witte (eds), *The Origins of Yahwism*, 145–56, BZAW 484; Berlin and Boston: W. de Gruyter.

Jöcken, P. (1977), *Das Buch Habakuk: Darstellung der Geschichte seiner kritischen Erforschung mit einer eigenen Beurteilung*, Bonner Biblische Beiträge 48; Cologne: Peter Hanstein Verlag.

Johnson, M. D. (1985), 'The Paralysis of Torah in Habakkuk I 4', *VT* 35: 257–66.

Jones, B. A. (1995), *The Formation of the Book of the Twelve: A Study in Text and Canon*, SBLDS 149; Atlanta: Scholars Press.

Jones, B. A. (2016), 'The Seventh-Century Prophets in Twenty-First Century Research', *CBR* 14: 129–75.

Kahn, D. (2009), 'The Historical Setting of Zephaniah's Oracles Against the Nations (Zeph 2:4-15)', in G. Galil, M. Geller and A. Millard (eds), *Homeland and Exile: FS B. Oded*, 439–53, VTSup 130; Leiden and Boston: Brill.

Kamionkowski, S. T. (2007), 'The "Problem" of Violence in Prophetic Literature: Definitions as the Real Problem', in D. A. Bernat and J. Klawans (eds), *Religion and Violence: The Biblical Heritage*, 38–46, Recent Research in Biblical Studies 2; Sheffield: Sheffield Phoenix Press.

Kapelrud, A. S. (1948), *Joel Studies*, Uppsala Universitets Arsskrift 4; Uppsala: Lundequist.

Kapelrud, A. S. (1975), *The Message of the Prophet Zephaniah: Morphology and Ideas*, Oslo: Universitetsforlaget.

Kelly, J. R. (2013), 'Joel, Jonah, and the YHWH Creed: Determining the Trajectory of the Literary Influence', *JBL* 132: 805–26.

Klawans, J. (with contributions from David A. Bernat) (2007), 'Introduction: Religion, Violence, and the Bible', in D. A. Bernat and J. Klawans (eds), *Religion and Violence: The Biblical Heritage*, 1–15, Recent Research in Biblical Studies 2; Sheffield: Sheffield Phoenix Press.

Ko, G. (2014), *Theodicy in Habakkuk*, Paternoster Biblical Monographs; Milton Keynes: Paternoster.

Koenen, K. (1994), *Heil den Gerechten — Unheil den Sündern!* BZAW, 229; Berlin: W. de Gruyter.

Kratz, R. G. (2015a), *The Prophets of Israel*, CSHB, 2; Winonan Lake: Eisenbrauns.

Kratz, R. G. (2015b), *Historical and Biblical Israel: The History, Tradition, and Archives of Israel and Judah*, Oxford: Oxford University Press.

Krinetzki, G. (1977) *Zefanjastudien. Motiv- und Traditionskritik + Kompositions- und Redaktionskritik*, Regensburger Studien zur Theologie 7; Frankfurt und Bern: P. Lang.

Lange, A. (2006), 'Literary Prophecy and Oracle Collection: A Comparison Between Judah and Greece in Persian Times', in M. H. Floyd and R. D. Haak (eds), *Prophets, Prophecy, and Prophetic Texts in Second Temple Judaism*, 248–75, New York and London: T&T Clark.

Lee, L. (2016), *Mapping Judah's Fate in Ezekiel's Oracles Against the Nations*, ANEM 15; Atlanta: SBL.

Legaspi, M. C. (2017), 'Opposition to Idolatry in the Book of Habakkuk', *VT* 67: 458–69.

Lemaire, A. (2010), 'Edom and the Edomites', in A. Lemaire and B. Halpern (eds), *The Book of Kings: Sources, Composition, Historiography and Reception*, 225–43, VTSup 129; Leiden and Boston: Brill.

Lescow, T. (1995), 'Die Komposition der Bücher Nahum und Habakuk', *Biblische Notizen* 77: 59–85.

Lescow, T. (1999), 'Die Komposition des Buches Obadja', *ZAW* 111: 380–98.

Leuenberger, M. (2010), 'Jhwhs Herkunft aus dem Süden: Archäologische Befunde — biblische Überlieferungen — historische Korrelationen', *ZAW* 122: 1–19.

Leuenberger, M. (2017), 'YHWH's Provenance from the South: A New Evaluation of the Arguments Pro and Contra', in J. van Oorschot and M. Witte (eds), *The Origins of Yahwism*, 157–79, BZAW 484; Berlin and Boston: W. de Gruyter.

Levin, C. (2011a), 'Zephaniah How This Book Became Prophecy', in L. L. Grabbe and M. Nissinen (eds), *Constructs of Prophecy in the Former and Latter Prophets and Other Texts*, 117–39, ANEM 4; Atlanta: SBL.

Levin, C. (2011b), 'Das "Vierprophetenbuch": Ein exegetischer Nachruf', *ZAW* 123: 221–35.

Limburg, J. (1988), *Hosea-Micah*, Interpretation; Atlanta: John Knox Press.

Lindblom, J. (1967), *Prophecy in Ancient Israel*, Oxford: Basil Blackwell.

Lindsay, J. (1976), 'The Babylonian Kings and Edom, 605-550 B.C.', *Palestine Exploration Quarterly* 108: 23–39.

Lo, A. (2011), 'Remnant Motif in Amos, Micah and Zephaniah', in J. A. Grant, A. Lo and G. J. Wenham (eds), *A God of Faithfulness: FS J.G. McConville*, 130–48, LHBOTS 538; London and New York: T&T Clark.

Lortie, C.R. (2016), *Mighty to Save: A Literary and Historical Study of Habakkuk 3 and Its Traditions*, Arbreiten zu Text und Sprache im Alten Testament 99; St. Ottilien: EOS.

Mack, R. (2011), *Neo-Assyrian Prophecy and the Hebrew Bible: Nahum, Habakkuk, and Zephaniah*, Perspectives on Hebrew Scriptures and its Contexts 14; Piscataway: Gorgias Press.

Marcus, D. (1994), 'Nonrecurring Doublets in the Book of Joel', *CBQ* 56: 56–67.

Markl, D. (2004), 'Hab 3 in intertextueller und kontextueller Sicht', *Biblica* 85: 99–108.

Mason, R. (1991), *Micah, Nahum, Obadiah*, Old Testament Guides; Sheffield: JSOT Press.

Mason, R. (1994), *Zephaniah, Habakkuk, Joel*, Old Testament Guides; Sheffield: JSOT Press.

Mathews, J. (2012), *Performing Habakkuk: Faithful Re-Enactment in the Midst of Crisis*, Eugene: Pickwick.

Mazar, A. (1990), *Archaeology of the Land of the Bible 10, 000-586 BCE*, New York: Doubleday.

Moseman, R. D. (2017), 'Habakkuk's Dialogue with Faithful Yahweh: A Transforming Experience', *Perspectives in Religious Studies* 44: 261–74.

Müller, A. K. (2008), *Gottes Zukunft: Die Möglichkeit der Rettung am Tag JHWHs nach dem Joelbuch*, WMANT 119; Neukirchen-Vluyn: Neukirchener Verlag.

Na'aman, N. (2007), 'Josiah and the Kingdom of Judah', in L. L. Grabbe (ed.), *Good Kings and Bad Kings: The Kingdom of Judah in the Seventh Century BCE*, 189–247, London and New York: T&T Clark.

Na'aman, N. (2016), 'The Prophecy of Obadiah in Historical Perspective', in B. Becking (ed.), *Obadiah*, 14–31, Readings; Sheffield: Sheffield Phoenix Press.

Neef, H.-D. (1999) 'Vom Gottesgericht zum universalen Heil: Komposition und Redaktion des Zephanjabuches', *ZAW* 111: 530–46.

Niehaus, J. (1993), 'Obadiah', in T. E. McComiskey (ed.), *The Minor Prophets* (Vol 2), 495–541, Grand Rapids: Baker.

Nissinen, M. (2000), 'Spoken, Written, Quoted, and Invented: Orality and Writtenness in Ancient Near Eastern Prophecy', in E. Ben Zvi and M. H. Floyd (eds), *Writings and Speech in Israelite and Ancient Near Easter Prophecy*, 235–71, SBLSS 10; Atlanta: SBL.

Nissinen, M. (2003), *Prophets and Prophecy in the Ancient Near East*, Writings from the Ancient World 12; Leiden and Boston: Brill.

Nissinen, M. (2017), *Ancient Prophecy: Near Eastern, Biblical, and Greek Perspectives*, Oxford: Oxford University Press.

Nogalski, J. D. (1993a), *Literary Precursors to the Book of the Twelve*, BZAW 217; Berlin and New York: W. de Gruyter.

Nogalski, J. D. (1993b), *Redactional Processes in the Book of the Twelve*, BZAW 218; Berlin and New York: W. de Gruyter.

Nogalski, J. D. (2000), 'Joel as "Literary Anchor" for the Book of the Twelve', in J. D. Nogalski and M. A. Sweeney (eds), *Reading and Hearing the Book of the Twelve*, 91–109, SBLSS 15; Atlanta: SBL.

Nogalski, J. D. (2011), *The Book of the Twelve* (2 Vols), Smyth & Helwys Bible Commentary; Macon: Smyth & Helwys.

O'Brien, J. M. (2004), *Nahum, Habakkuk, Zephaniah, Haggai, Zechariah, Malachi*, Abingdon Old Testament Commentary; Nashville: Abingdon.

O'Brien, J. M. (2008), *Challenging Prophetic Metaphor: Theology and Ideology in the Prophets*, Louisville and London: Westminster John Knox Press.

O'Brien, J. M. and Franke, C. (eds) (2010), *The Aesthetics of Violence in the Prophets*, LHBOTS 517; New York and London: T&T Clark

Oeming, M. (1987), 'Gericht Gottes und Geschichteder Völker nach Zef 3, 1–13', *Theologische Quartalschrift* 167: 289–300.

Ogden, G. S. (1982), 'Prophetic Oracles Against Foreign Nations and Psalms of Communal Lament: The Relationship of Psalm 137 to Jeremiah 49: 7-22 and Obadiah', *JSOT* 24: 89–97.

Ogden, G. S. (1983), 'Joel 4 and Prophetic Responses to National Laments', *JSOT* 26: 97–106.

Ogden, G. S. (1987), 'A Commentary on the Book of Joel', in G. S. Ogden and R. R. Deutsch (eds), *A Promise of Hope - A Call to Obedience: Joel & Malachi*, 3–60, ITC; Grand Rapids and Edinburgh: Eerdmans.

O'Neal, G. M. (2007), *Interpreting Habakkuk as Scripture: An Application of the Canonical Approach of Brevard S. Childs*, Studies in Biblical Literature 9; New York: Peter Lang.

Parpola, S. (1997), *Assyrian Prophecies*, SAA 9; Helsinki: Helsinki University Press.

Perlitt, L. (2004), *Die Propheten Nahum, Habakuk, Zephanja*, ATD 25.1; Göttingen: Vandenhoeck & Ruprecht.

Petersen, D. L. (1977), *Late Israelite Prophecy: Studies in Deutero-Prophetic Literature and in Chronicles*, SBLMS 23; Missoula: Scholars Press.

Petersen, D. L. (2011), 'Israel and the Nations in the Later Latter Prophets', in L. L. Grabbe and M. Nissinen (eds), *Constructs of Prophecy in the Former and Latter Prophets and Other Texts*, 157–64, ANEM 4; Atlanta: SBL.

Pfeiffer, H. (2005), *Jahwes Kommen von Süden: Jdc 5; Hab 3; Dtn 33 und Ps 68 in ihrem literatur- und theologiegeschichtlichen Umfeld*, FRLANT 211; Göttingen: Vandenhoeck & Ruprecht.

Pfeiffer, H. (2017), 'The Origin of YHWH and Its Attestation', in J. van Oorschot and M. Witte (eds), *The Origins of Yahwism*, 115–44, BZAW 484; Berlin and Boston: W. de Gruyter.

Pinker, A. (2007), 'Habakkuk 2.4: An Ethical Paradigm or a Political Observation', *JSOT* 32: 91–112.

Plöger, O. (1968), *Theocracy and Eschatology*, trans. S. Rudman, Oxford: Basil Blackwell.

Pons, M. V. (2014), 'The Origin of the Name Sepharad: A New Interpretation', *Journal of Semitic Studies* 59: 297–313.

Prinsloo, G. T. M. (1999), 'Reading Habakkuk as a Literary Unit: Exploring the Possibilities', *OTE* 12: 515–35.

Prinsloo, G. T. M. (2001), 'Yahweh the Warrior: An Intertextual Reading of Habakkuk 3', *OTE* 14: 475–93.

Prinsloo, G. T. M. (2002), 'Reading Habakkuk 3 in Its Literary Context: A Worthwhile Exercise or a Futile Attempt?' *Journal for Semitics* 11: 83–111.

Prinsloo, G. T. M. (2004), 'Habakkuk 1 - a Dialogue? Ancient Unit Delimiters in Dialogue with Modern Critical Interpretation', *OTE* 17: 621–45.

Prinsloo, W. S. (1985), *The Theology of the Book of Joel*, BZAW, 163; Berlin and New York: W. de Gruyter.

Prinsloo, W. S. (1992), 'The Unity of the Book of Joel', *ZAW* 104: 66–81.

Raabe, P. R. (1995), 'Why Prophetic Oracles against the Nations?' in A. B. Beck, A. H. Bartelt, P. R. Raabe and C. A. Franke (eds), *Fortunate the Eyes That See: FS D.N. Freedman*, 236–57, Grand Rapids and Cambridge: Eerdmans.

Raabe, P. R. (1996), *Obadiah*, AB 24D; New York: Doubleday.

Radine, J. (2010), *The Book of Amos in Emergent Judah*, Forschungen zum Alten Testament 45; Tübingen: Mohr Siebeck.

Redditt, P. L. (1986), 'The Book of Joel and Peripheral Prophecy', *CBQ* 48: 225–40.

Rendtorff, R. (2000), 'How to Read the Book of the Twelve as a Theological Unity', in J. D. Nogalski and M. A. Sweeney (eds), *Reading and Hearing the Book of the Twelve*, 75–87, SBLSS 15; Atlanta: SBL.

Renkema, J. (2003), *Obadiah*, HCOT; Leuven: Peeters.

Renz, T. (2013), 'An Emendation of Hab 2:4a in the Light of Hab 1:5', *JHS* 13: Article 8.

Renz, T. (2018), 'Habakkuk and Its Co-Texts', in H. Wenzel (ed.), *The Book of the Twelve: An Anthology of Prophetic Books or The Result of Complex Redactional Processes?* 13–36, Göttingen: V&R unipress.

Rice, G. (1979), 'The African Roots of the Prophet Zephaniah', *Journal of Religious Thought* 36: 21–31.

Ro, J. U.-S. (2002), *Die sogenannte 'Armenfrömmigkeit' im nachexilischen Israel*, BZAW 322; Berlin and New York: W. de Gruyter.

Roberts, J. J. M. (1991), *Nahum, Habakkuk, and Zephaniah: A Commentary*, OTL; Louisville: Westminster/John Knox Press.

Robertson, O. P. (1990), *The Books of Nahum, Habakkuk, and Zephaniah*, NICOT; Grand Rapids: Eerdmans.

Roth, M. (2005), *Israel und die Völker im Zwölfprophetenbuch: Eine Untersuchung zu den Büchern Joel, Jona, Micha und Nahum*, FRLANT 210; Göttingen: Vandenhoeck & Ruprecht.

Rudolph, W. (1971), *Joel — Amos — Obadja — Jona*, KAT 13.2; Gütersloh: Gerd Mohn.

Rudolph, W. (1975), *Micha — Nahum — Habakuk — Zephanja*, KAT 13.3; Gütersloh: Gerd Mohn.

Ryou, D. H. (1995), *Zephaniah's Oracles Against the Nations: A Synchronic and Diachronic Study of Zephaniah 2:1-3:8*, BIS 13; Leiden: Brill.

Schaper, J. (2005), 'Exilic and Post-Exilic Prophecy and the Orality/Literacy Problem', *VT* 55: 324–42.

Schart, A. (1998), *Die Entstehung des Zwölfprophetenbuchs: Neubearbeitungen von Amos im Rahmen schriftenübergreifender Redaktionsprozesse*, BZAW 260; Berlin and New York: W. de Gruyter.

Schlenke, B. and Weimar, P. (2009a), '"Hab Mitleid, JHWH, mit deinem Volk!" (Joel 2,17): Zu Struktur und Komposition von Joel (Teil 1)', *BZ* 53: 1–28.

Schlenke, B. and Weimar, P. (2009b) '"Und JHWH eiferte für sein Land und erbarmte sich seines Volkes" (Joel 2.18): Zu Struktur und Komposition von Joel (Teil 2)', *BZ* 53: 212–37.

Schneider, D. A. (1979), *The Unity of the Book of the Twelve*, Unpublished PhD Dissertation, Yale University.

Schupak, N. (2001), 'The God from Teman and the Egyptian Sun God: A Reconsideration of Habakkuk 3.3-7', *Journal of the Ancient Near Eastern Society* 28: 97–116.

Schwesig, P.-G. (2006), *Die Rolle der Tag-JHWHs-Dichtungen im Dodekapropheton*, BZAW 366; Berlin and New York: W. de Gruyter.

Seitz, C. R. (2016), *Joel*, ITC; London: Bloomsbury.

Seybold, K. (1985), *Satirische Prophetie: Studien zum Buch Zefanja*, Stuttgarter Bibelstudien 120; Stuttgart: Verlag Katholisches Bibelwerk.

Seybold, K. (1991), *Nahum, Habakuk, Zephanja*, Zürcher Bibelkommentare AT 24.2; Zürich: Theologischer Verlag.

Simkins, R. (1991), *Yahweh's Activity in History and the Nature of the Book of Joel*, Ancient Near Eastern Texts and Studies 10; Lewiston: Mellen.

Smith, J. M. P. (1911), *Micah, Zephaniah and Nahum*, ICC; Edinburgh: T&T Clark.

Smith, R. L. (1984), *Micah-Malachi*, WBC 32; Waco: Word.

Snyman, G. F. (2016), 'Obadiah and the Hermeneutic of Vulnerability', in B. Becking (ed.), *Obadiah*, 45–63, Readings; Sheffield: Sheffield Phoenix Press.

Snyman, S. D. (1989), 'Cohesion in the Book of Obadiah', *ZAW* 101: 59–71.

Snyman, S. D. (2003), 'Non-Violent Prophet and Violent God in the Book of Habakkuk', *OTE* 16: 422–34.

Stern, E. (2001), *Archaeology of the Land of the Bible: The Assyrian, Babylonian, and Persian Period (732-332 B.C.E.)*, New York: Doubleday.

Strazicich, J. (2007), *Joel's Use of Scripture and the Scripture's Use of Joel: Appropriation and Resignification in Second Temple Judaism and Early Christianity*, BIS 82; Leiden and Boston: Brill.

Striek, M. (1999), *Das vordeuteronomistische Zephanjabuch*, Beiträge zur biblischen Exegese und Theologie 29; Frankfurt: Peter Lang.

Stökl, J. (2012), *Prophecy in the Ancient Near East: A Philological and Sociological Comparison*, Culture and History of the Ancient Near East 56; Leiden and Boston: Brill.

Stuart, D. (1987), *Hosea-Jonah*, WBC 31; Waco: Word.

Stulman, L. (2007), 'Reading the Prophets as Meaning-Making Literature for Communities under Siege', *Horizons in Biblical Theology* 29: 153–75.

Sweeney, M. A. (1991a), 'Structure, Genre, and Intent in the Book of Habakkuk', *VT* 41: 63–83.

Sweeney, M. A. (1991b), 'Form-Critical Reassessment of the Book of Zephaniah', *CBQ* 53: 388–408.

Sweeney, M. A. (2000a), *The Twelve Prophets*, Berit Olam; Collegeville: Liturgical Press.

Sweeney, M. A. (2000b), 'Sequence and Interpretation in the Book of the Twelve', in J. D. Nogalski and M. A. Sweeney (eds), *Reading and Hearing the Book of the Twelve*, 49–64, SBLSS 15; Atlanta: SBL.

Sweeney, M. A. (2001), *King Josiah of Judah: The Lost Messiah of Israel*, Oxford: Oxford University Press.

Sweeney, M. A. (2003a), *Zephaniah*, Hermeneia; Minneapolis: Fortress.

Sweeney, M. A. (2003b), 'The Place and Function of Joel in the Book of the Twelve', in P. L. Redditt and A. Schart (eds), *Thematic Threads in the Book of the Twelve*, 133–54, BZAW 325; Berlin and New York: W. de Gruyter.

Szeles, M. E. (1987), *Wrath and Mercy: A Commentary on the Books of Habakkuk and Zephaniah*, ITC; Grand Rapids and Edinburgh: Eerdmans and Handsel.

Tebes, J. M. (2011), 'The Edomite Involvement in the Destruction of the First Temple: A Case of Stab-in-the-Back Tradition?' *JSOT* 36: 219–55.

Tebes, J. M. (2014), 'Socio-Economic Fluctuations and Chiefdom Formation in Edom, the Negev and the Hejaz During the First Millennium BCE', in J. M. Tebes (ed.), *Unearthing the Wilderness: Studies on the Archaeology of the Negev and Edom in the Iron Age*, 1–29, Ancient Near Eastern Studies Supplement 45; Leuven: Peeters.

Thomas, H. A. (2018), *Habakkuk*, The Two Horizons Old Testament Commentary; Grand Rapids: Eerdmans.

Thompson, M. E. W. (1993), 'Prayer, Oracle and Theophany: The Book of Habakkuk', *Tyndale Bulletin* 44: 33–53.

Timmer, D. C. (2015a), *The Non-Israelite Nations in the Book of the Twelve: Thematic Coherence and the Diachronic-Synchronic Relationship in the Minor Prophets*, BIS 135; Leiden and Boston: Brill.

Timmer, D. C. (2015b), 'The Non-Israelite Nations in Zephaniah: Conceptual Coherence and the Relationship of the Parts to the Whole', in M. J. Boda, M. H. Floyd and C. M. Toffelmire (eds), *The Book of the Twelve and the New Form Criticism*, 245–63, ANEM 10; Atlanta: SBL.

Troxel, R. L. (2015a), *Joel: Scope, Genre(s), and Meaning*, CSHB 6; Winona Lake: Eisenbrauns.

Troxel, R. L. (2015b), 'The Fate of Joel in the Redaction of the Twelve', *CBR* 13: 152–74.

Uehlinger, C. (1996), 'Astralkultpriester und Fremdgekleidete, Kanaanvolk und Silberwäger: Zur Verknüpfung von Kult- und Sozialkritik in Zef 1', in W. Dietrich and M. Schwantes (eds), *Der Tag wird kommen: Ein interkontextuelles Gespräch über das Buch des Propheten Zefanja*, 49–83, Stuttgart: Verlag Katholisches Bibelwerk GmbH.

Uehlinger, C. (2007), 'Was There a Cult Reform under King Josiah? The Case for a Well Grounded Minimum', in L. L. Grabbe (ed.), *Good Kings and Bad Kings: The Kingdom of Judah in the Seventh Century BCE*, 279–316, London and New York: T&T Clark.

Van der Toorn, K. (2000), 'From the Oral to the Written: The Case of Old Babylonian Prophecy', in E. Ben Zvi and M. H. Floyd (eds), *Writings and Speech in Israelite and Ancient Near Easter Prophecy*, 219–34, SBLSS 10; Atlanta: SBL.

Van Leeuwen, C. (1974), 'The Prophecy of the Yom YHWH in Amos v 18–20', in J. Barr (ed.), *Language and Meaning: Studies in Hebrew Language and Biblical Exegesis*, 113–34, OTS 19; Leiden: Brill.

Vlaardingerbroek, J. (1999), *Zephaniah*, HCOT; Leuven: Peeters.

Watts, J. D. W. (1969), *Obadiah*, Grand Rapids: Eerdmans.

Watts, J. D. W. (1975), *The Books of Joel, Obadiah, Jonah, Nahum, Habakkuk and Zephaniah*, Cambridge: Cambridge University Press.

Watts, J. W. (1996), 'Psalmody in Prophecy: Habakkuk 3 in Context', in J. W. Watts and P. R. House (eds), *Forming Prophetic Literature: FS J. D.W. Watts*, 209–23, JSOTSup 235; Sheffield: Sheffield Academic Press.

Weigl, M. (1994), *Zefanja und das 'Israel der Armen': eine Untersuchung zur Theologie des Buches Zefanja*, Österreichische biblische Studien 13; Klosterneuburg: Osterreichisches Katholisches Bibelwerk.

Weis, R. D. (1992), 'Oracle: Old Testament', *Anchor Bible Dictionary* 5: 28–9.

Welch, E. L. (2013), 'The Roots of Anger: An Economic Perspective on Zephaniah's Oracle Against the Philistines', *VT* 63: 471–85.

Wellhausen, J. (1898), *Die kleinen Propheten übersetz und erklärt*, 3rd edn, Berlin: Georg Reimer.

Whitehead, P. (2016), 'Habakkuk and the Problem of Suffering: Theodicy Deferred', *Journal of Theological Interpretation* 10: 265–81.

Williams, D. L. (1963), 'The Date of Zephaniah', *JBL* 82: 77–88.

Williamson, H. G. M. (1982), 'Joel', in G. W. Bromiley (ed.), *The International Standard Bible Encyclopedia* (Vol 2), 1076–80, Grand Rapids: Eerdmans.

Wilson, R. R. (1980), *Prophecy and Society in Ancient Israel*, Philadelphia: Fortress.

Wolff, H. W. (1977), *Joel and Amos*, trans. W. Janzen, S. D. McBride, Jr. and C. A. Muenchow, Hermeneia; Philadelphia: Fortress Press.

Wolff, H. W. (1986), *Obadiah and Jonah*, trans. M. Kohl, Minneapolis: Augsburg.

Wöhrle, J. (2006), *Die frühen Sammlungen des Zwölfprophetenbuches: Entstehung und Komposition*, BZAW 360; Berlin and New York: W. de Gruyter.

Wöhrle, J. (2008a), *Der Abschluss des Zwölfprophetenbuches: Buchübergreifende Redaktionsprozesse in den späten Sammlungen*, BZAW 389; Berlin and New York: W. de Gruyter.

Wöhrle, J. (2008b), '"No Future for the Proud Exultant Ones": The Exilic Book of the Four Prophets (Hos., Am., Mic., Zeph.) as a Concept Opposed to the Deuteronomistic History', *VT* 58: 608–27.

Wöhrle, J. (2010), 'Joel and the Formation of the Book of the Twelve', *Biblical Theology Bulletin* 40: 127–37.

Zehnder, M. and Hagelia, H. (eds) (2013), *Encountering Violence in the Bible*, The Bible in the Modern World 55; Sheffield: Sheffield Phoenix Press.

General subject index

Africa 55, 105
allegory 53
apocalyptic 14, 25–6, 29, 33, 35, 37, 68,
    76–7, 102, 119
Arad ostraca 46–7
Assyria 8, 28, 32, 46, 66, 69, 97, 102,
    104, 108–10, 112, 116–17
Assyrian prophecy 67, 91, 103

Babylon 8, 28, 32, 45–7, 52, 61–4,
    65–71, 75, 81–3, 98, 109–10,
    112–13

chaos monster 34–5, 50, 64
composite texts 33–4, 42–4, 99–103,
    115–21
  criteria 15–16, 43, 70–1, 73–6,
    91–5
  hermeneutical significance 16–17,
    29–30, 35–7, 78, 81–2, 118–21
context
  canonical 22, 69, 84–5
  literary 6–7, 9, 22
  historical 6, 19, 22, 45–7, 52, 54, 65,
    69, 84, 91–2, 119–20
cult 15, 16, 20, 21, 24–5, 26, 29, 50–1,
    72, 75–6, 78
cultic prophet 24–5, 50–1, 71–2

Day of the Lord 7–9, 14–17, 20, 25,
    27–30, 31, 33, 34–7, 43–4, 89–90,
    93–4, 99–103, 111–13
deconstruction 83
deuteronomistic 69, 102, 110–13

Edom 15, 27, 45–7, 50, 52–3, 77,
    109–10

Egypt 15, 19, 27–8, 50, 66, 68, 77, 97,
    104, 109, 113
empire 70–1, 81–2

final form 60–2, 80–1, 118
Four, book of 7, 111–12

genres
  complaint 60–1
  didactic 29–30, 90
  drama 89–90
  exhortation 90
  lament 13–15, 24, 32–3, 66–7, 73
  literary-predictive 91
  liturgy 24, 29, 32–3, 49
  OAN 49–50, 92–4, 104, 107–10
  oracle 60, 90–1
  prayer 63–4, 73
  prophetic book 24–30, 89–92
  vision 61–2, 74, 76
  woe 62–3, 70–1, 82
God
  female images 84–5
  indescribable 84
  mystery 80
  warrior 63–4, 83–4

hope 15, 25, 34–7, 115–20

identity, communal 26, 29–30, 53, 90
idolatry 82, 102
intertextuality 8–9, 21, 27–8, 41–2,
    102, 108, 117–18

Jehoiakim 6, 63, 66, 68–70, 104
Josiah 6, 8, 19, 66, 69–70, 97–8, 102–5,
    109–13, 119

Kenite hypothesis   76

literary prophecy   91–2
literary skill   16, 44, 100–2
literary structures   13–15, 59, 92–5,
        99–100

moral creation-order   81–2

Nabonidus   47
nations   7, 13–17, 21, 24–8, 32–6, 43–4,
        50, 62, 70–1, 75, 77, 93–4, 107–13,
        117–19

oral
    prophecy   67, 103–5, 112–13
    tradition   28

period
    exilic   20, 45–8, 49–51, 52–3, 66–7,
        72, 76, 90, 109–12, 117
    Hellenistic   26, 68, 77
    Persian   20–2, 67
    post-exilic   25–6, 48, 98–9, 116, 120
    pre-exilic (monarchic)   19–20, 43, 49,
        65–6, 97–8, 108–10, 112–13, 116–17

pre-monarchic   76–8
politics   67, 68, 112–13
poor   70, 74, 81, 116–17, 120
post-colonial   55, 81–2

reader-response   36–7, 54–5, 61, 80–1,
        84–5, 95, 120–1
redaction criticism, *see* composite texts
remnant   93, 115–17
repentance   28, 29–30, 35, 94–5, 120–1

Sabeans   21
Satire   104
scribal prophecy   26, 27–9, 50, 67–8,
        90–2, 98–9, 102–3, 108
Sepharad   48
social justice   63, 66–7, 69, 70–1, 81,
        102, 116–17

Teman   77–8
theodicy   79–81
theophany   63, 77
Twelve, book of   6–9, 21–2, 28, 42, 49,
        67, 69, 76, 111–12

violence   45, 54, 60–3, 69–71, 80, 82–5

Index of scripture references

Genesis
2.10-14   108
ch. 10   108
ch. 11   111, 117
11.1-9   108

Exodus
5.7   116
8.18   27
10.2   27
10.6   27
10.14   27

Deuteronomy
ch. 33   76

Judges
ch. 5   76, 77

2 Kings
chs 18–20   105
chs 22–23   97, 104
ch 23   102, 111
23.4,5   102
23.12   102

Ezra
3.8   20
5.8   20

Psalms
4.1   75
6.1   75
7.1   63
17   75
54.1   75

55.1   75
67.1   75
68   76
86   75
90   75
102   75
137.7-9   46
142   75

Isaiah
2.4   28
2.12-17   104
ch. 13   28
chs 13–23   49
13.2-16   27
13.4   27
13.5   27
13.6   27
13.8   27
13.9   27
13.10   27
13.13   27
13.16   27
18.1, 7   118
ch. 34   46
45.6   109
46.9   109
63.1-7   46, 77

Jeremiah
chs 4–6   27
5.15-17   61
13.19   46
22.13   63
40.11   46
46–51   49

49.7-16   50
49.14-16   41–2
49.9   41–2

Lamentations
4.21-22   46
5.9   46

Ezekiel
ch. 25   46
chs 25–32   49–50
ch. 30   28
ch. 35   46
36.4-5   46
chs 38–39   27
47.1-12   27

Hosea
1.1   111

Joel
1.1–2.11   13–14
1.1–2.27   13–17, 22, 29,
            36
1.2   27
1.2-3   29
1.2-12   14
1.2-20   14
1.2–2.17   13–16
1.3   27
1.4   27, 28, 31
1.4-20   33
1.5   16
1.5-13   16, 27
1.5-20   34
1.5–2.11   27

1.5–2.17	29	2.25	14, 27, 31	4.6-11	108
1.6	14, 31, 32	2.27	16, 27, 36	4.6-12	108
1.6-7	14, 33	2.28	15, 35	4.12	108
1.6-8	34	2.28-29	25	5.14-15	102
1.9	21	2.28-32	14–15, 25–6,	5.18-20	35. 102, 104
1.13	21		29, 34, 36	9.12	46
1.13-20	14	2.28–3.21	14–17, 22,	9.13	28
1.14	16, 21		26, 29, 33, 35,		
1.15	16, 27, 28, 31,		36–7	Obadiah	
	33	2.30	25	1–5	41–2
1.15-20	16	2.31	16, 31	1–7	43
1.16	21	2.32	27	1–9	43
1.17-20	31	3.1	14, 16	1–14	41, 43–4, 47,
1.20	16	3.1-3	15, 19		51
2.1	27, 31	3.2	21	1–15	43
2.1-9	34, 35	3.3	27	2–4	44
2.1-11	14, 16, 27, 28,	3.4	27	5	42, 43
	31, 32, 33	3.4-8	15, 21	5–7	48
2.1-14	33	3.7	27	7–9	47
2.2	27	3.8	21	8	44, 47
2.3	27	3.9	16	8–18	43
2.4-9	32	3.9-15	15	9	44
2.6	27	3.9-16	25	10–14	43, 45
2.7	16, 21	3.10	28	11	27, 45
2.9	21, 27	3.11b	14	11–14	44
2.10	16, 27	3.13	32	12–14	45, 54
2.11	16, 31, 35	3.14	16, 31	15	27, 41, 43–4,
2.11-17	14	3.15	16, 25		47, 48, 51
2.12-14	28	3.16	14, 25, 28	15–21	43
2.12-17	13–14, 29, 33	3.16-18	15	16	43, 44
2.12b-13a	14	3.16-21	25	16–17	43
2.15-17a	16	3.17	16, 21	16–21	41, 43, 48
2.16	16	3.18	16, 25, 27–8,	17	27
2.17	14, 21, 32		32	18	43, 54
2.17b	16	3.19	19, 27	19	44
2.18-19a	29	3.19-20	46	19–20	43
2.18-27	13–14, 33	3.19-21	15	19–21	43
2.18–3.21	13–16			20	48
2.19-27	16, 29	Amos		21	44
2.20	14, 27, 31,	chs 1–2	49		
	32	1.2	28	Jonah	
2.21-23	14	1.3–2.16	100, 108	3.9	28
2.23-24	31	1.11-12	46	4.2	28

Micah

1.1	111
4.3	28

Habakkuk

1.1	60, 63, 71
1.1–2.20	63
1.2	74, 82
1.2-4	59–61, 66–7, 69–71, 79
1.2-17	59, 61, 75
1.2–2.1	80
1.2–2.4	59–61, 711.3 82
1.4	68, 74
1.5	60, 73
1.5-6	61
1.5-11	60–1, 66–9, 71, 79, 83
1.5-12	67
1.5-17	73
1.5–2.17	75
1.6	62, 65, 67–8, 72
1.9	68, 82
1.11	82
1.12	71
1.12-13	66, 79
1.12-14	70
1.12-17	60–1, 69
1.13	67, 68, 71, 74
1.14-17	66–7
1.15-17	68, 71, 74
1.16	82
1.17	70
2.1	70, 71, 74
2.1-3	66
2.1-4	59, 61–2, 67
2.1-20	59
2.2-4	70
2.2-20	80
2.3	62
2.3-4	74

2.3-5	80
2.4	61–2, 66, 80
2.4(-5)	61–2
2.5	74, 82
2.5-20	59, 68
2.5-19	66
2.6	62, 63, 67, 70, 71, 75
2.6-7	71, 82
2.6-11	82
2.6-16	71
2.6-17	70
2.6-19	70
2.6-20	61, 75, 80
2.7	62
2.7-8	62, 71
2.8	62, 71, 82
2.9	62, 63, 67, 70
2.9-10	74
2.10	75
2.12	67, 70
2.15	62, 67, 70, 74
2.15-16	82
2.16	62, 75, 82
2.17	62, 82
2.18-19	82
2.19	62, 67, 70
2.20	66, 82
3.1	71, 75
3.1-2	77
3.1-19	59, 63–4, 80
3.2	73, 74, 75, 77
3.2-15	75
3.2-16	76
3.3	75, 77–8
3.3-4	63
3.3-7	77
3.3-12	77
3.3-15	61, 74
3.4	63
3.5-15	77
3.7	75
3.8-15	77

3.9	75
3.12-14	73
3.13	64, 74, 75, 77
3.13-14	66, 74
3.13-16	77
3.14	74, 78
3.14-19	74
3.16	71, 73, 74, 75, 77, 78
3.16-17	76
3.16-19	74, 80
3.17	64, 74, 75, 78
3.17-19	66
3.18-19	76, 77
3.19	74, 75

Zephaniah

1.1	111
1.1-18	93
1.1–2.3	95, 100, 103, 107–8
1.1–3.8	95, 99–100, 108, 110–13
1.1–3.10	99, 110–11
1.1–3.13	99
1.2	101
1.2-18	89, 94, 95, 99, 102, 111
1.2–2.3	92, 93, 100–3, 104, 105
1.2-3	94, 99, 100–2
1.3	101
1.3–3.8	112
1.4	101
1.4-5	102
1.4-6	102, 111
1.4-16	99, 100, 103
1.4–2.3	101
1.6	94
1.7	99, 101
1.7–2.4	103, 111
1.8	100, 102
1.9	100

1.11	101–2	2.4–3.5	100, 108	3.6-7	112
1.12	99, 100	2.4–3.8	95, 108	3.6-8	89, 94–5, 100
1.14	101	2.5	100	3.6-20	93
1.14-16	89, 94, 99,	2.5-6	109	3.7	93, 112
	100, 102, 103	2.5-7	108	3.8	93, 100, 108,
1.15-16	101–2	2.5-15	94		112–13, 118,
1.17	101	2.5–3.5	95		121
1.17-18	99	2.7	93, 95,	3.8-10	111
1.18	93, 94, 99,		115–17	3.9	118
	101–2, 112	2.8-9	100, 103, 108,	3.9-10	89, 93,
ch. 2	49		109		117–19
2.1	94, 101–2,	2.8-10	109, 117	3.9-13	94, 118
	115–16	2.9	109, 115–17	3.9-20	93–4, 95,
2.1-3	89, 94–5, 100,	2.9-10	93, 95		115–20
	101–2, 108,	2.11	115, 117–19	3.11-13	89, 93, 95,
	118, 121	2.12	100, 108, 109,		115–17
2.1-4	94, 95		117	3.14	94
2.1–3.5	93	2.12-14	109	3.14-15	117, 119
2.1–3.8	100	2.13-14	109, 113	3.14-20	89, 93, 94,
2.1–3.13	94	2.13-15	100, 108–9,		119–21
2.2	100, 101		113, 117		
2.2-3	94	2.14	116	Zechariah	
2.3	94, 101, 102,	3.1-4	104	chs 9–14	27
	108, 112–13,	3.1-5	89, 95, 100,		
	115–17, 121		108	Malachi	
2.4	94, 108, 109	3.1-8	92–3, 95, 119	1.1-4	48
2.4-5	103, 109	3.1-13	94, 118		
2.4-6	100, 109	3.1-20	92	Acts	
2.4-7	109, 113, 117	3.2	93, 112	2.1-4	35
2.4-15	89, 92, 93,	3.4	113	2.17	35
	94, 100, 104,	3.5	111	2.17-21	35
	107–10, 112	3.6	113	2.20	35

www.ingramcontent.com/pod-product-compliance
Ingram Content Group UK Ltd.
Pitfield, Milton Keynes, MK11 3LW, UK
UKHW022129020325
455697UK00001B/47